THE COMPLETE BOOK OF

HEATING WITH

WOOD

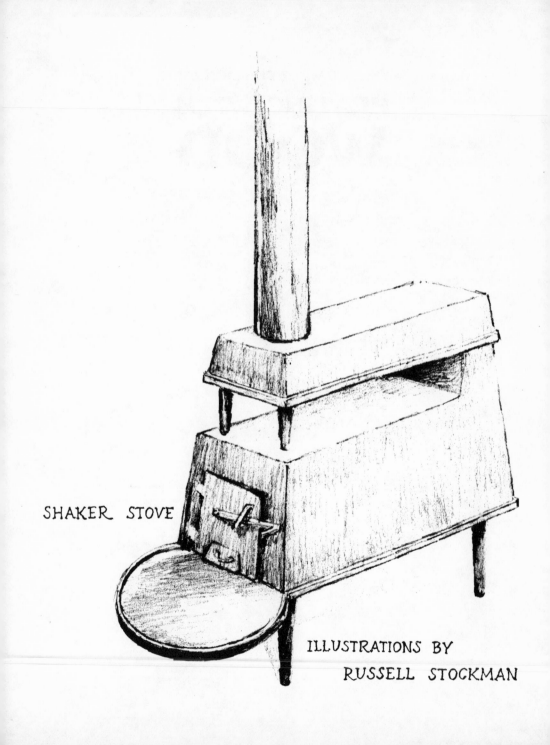

SHAKER STOVE

ILLUSTRATIONS BY
RUSSELL STOCKMAN

THE COMPLETE BOOK OF
HEATING WITH
WOOD

LARRY GAY

GARDEN WAY PUBLISHING · Charlotte, Vermont 05445

Published in the United States by Garden Way Publishing, Charlotte, Vermont 05445.

Tenth Printing, March 1980

Library of Congress Catalog Card Number: 74-83144
International Standard Book Number: 0-88266-036-5

Thanks are due:

*the thoughtful people who organized
the Montpelier Conference on
Alternate Sources of Energy,
before the energy crisis;*

*Professor Jay Shelton of Williams College,
whose knowledge of physics
and interest in wood heat
helped nip some frightful errors in the bud;*

*and Benjamin Franklin,
for his many helpful insights
and general perspicacity.*

CONTENTS

A tree is Nature's solar energy
converter and storage device.

It seems easier to destroy in greed
or to adopt the hands-off attitude
of the sentimentalist
than to establish a harmonious relationship
with the forest.

FUELWOOD
AND THE
ENVIRONMENT

Anyone advocating the use of wood as fuel has quite a bit of explaining to do. Americans worry about their forests and wonder what would happen to them if everyone heated with wood. Shouldn't we follow the advice on the shopping bags and save a tree? Besides, isn't wood a dirty fuel?

The answers to these questions are: 1. *there is right now an abundance of fuelwood which, if spread around, would be enough to heat at least half, and probably all, the houses in the country year-in, year-out without depleting the forests;* 2. *wood is a clean fuel if burned completely;* 3. *the products of incomplete combustion can be harmful, but are similar to the products of natural decay for which there are natural scavengers;* and 4. *everyone isn't going to heat with wood anyway.*

But the burden of proof is clearly on us and we want to answer the skeptics as best we can. Our answer goes like this: A century after Darwin it is, unfortunately, necessary to remind ourselves occasionally that we are part of the natural process. Like other species, we are dependent on the world's resources and must exploit them to survive. Among fuel resources wood is unique in that it is renewable. It is, like coal and oil, a source of energy that came to earth from the sun. The tree is nature's solar converter and energy storage device all in one.

There was a time when much more of the earth was covered with trees than now. Through over-cutting and subsequent soil depletion, much of China and the Mediterranean region are barren where forests once stood. In Europe, Asia and North America vast forests have been replaced with cropland. Thus the amount of timber standing today is far less than before the dramatic expansion of the human species.

Forests increasing

But now, thanks mainly to changes in technology, forests are once again on the increase, in spite of soaring paper and plywood use. Look at the heels of your shoes. Instead of hard maple they are more apt to be plastic or rubber. The siding on your house may be aluminum, the dashboard in your car isn't a board at all, and your refrigerator is almost certainly not wooden. Forests once provided power for steam boats, railroad trains, and many industries. The demand for railroad ties, although up, is hardly what it once was; the wood distillation industry has been virtually eliminated by competition from petrochemicals; hickory smoke for bacon is made in a chemical plant; and charcoal, once vital to the iron industry, is now used for little more than the backyard barbecue.

Another reason for the comeback of trees that is not so apparent is the large amount of carbon dioxide liberated to the atmosphere by the burning of fossil fuels.* But there are environmental mechanisms on a grand scale for absorbing some of the excess carbon dioxide. One of these is dissolution in the oceans; another is photosynthesis.

Remember from high school biology that the photosynthetic reaction is: *light energy + carbon dioxide + water = sugar + oxygen*. Sugar is the chemical precursor of the structural components of wood, roughly two-thirds of which is cellulose and one-third lignin. The chemical equation for photosynthesis tells us, among other things, that additional amounts of carbon dioxide enhance the growth of plants when light and water are abundant. Owners of commercial greenhouses make good use of this fact on a small scale. On the global scale man is inadvertently stimulating the growth of forests by adding tremendous amounts of carbon dioxide to the atmosphere from the burning of fossil fuels.

CO_2 promotes growth

Add to this the hundreds of thousands of acres of marginal farmland in the East reverting to forests because of competition from agribusiness on the prairies, and it is easy to see

---

* This extra carbon dioxide tends to raise the temperature of the earth by hindering the escape of radiant energy to outer space.[1]

that the total amount of wood in the United States is increasing every year. Occasionally we read about lumber and paper shortages in the newspaper; whatever the reason, it is not because we are running out of wood, although there may be shortages of certain species, especially of high quality and large size.

Individual decisions about using wood for fuel must be made on the basis of local conditions, but it is, nevertheless, of general interest to estimate the amount of wood potentially available as fuel right now. We do this in Table I, which is based on a recent report from the U. S. Forest Service.[2]

Eastern forests

Perhaps the most striking fact in the table is the amount of growth occurring in eastern forests every year. Even after timber cut and natural mortality have been taken into account, there is still a net annual growth of 4884 million cubic feet (61 million cords) of hardwoods and 2891 million cubic feet (36 million cords) of softwoods in the East. More than two-thirds of the tremendous growth of eastern hardwoods, which make preferable fuelwood, is in the heavily populated Middle Atlantic and Central states.

The manufacturing wastes are about 60 per cent shavings and sawdust, which require special burning equipment if they are to be used as fuel. The logging wastes are mainly tops—that is, what is left after the lower trunks are hauled to the mill—but in this category are also trees knocked over and damaged in logging. In the Mortality column are losses from old age, disease, blowdown and fire.

TABLE I

Potential Fuelwood Available per Year by Region
(millions of cubic feet)

	Manufacturing Residues		Logging Residues		Mortality		Net Growth	
	Hard	Soft	Hard	Soft	Hard	Soft	Hard	Soft
Northeast	71	24	125	52	357	208	1153	477
North Central	70	7	97	9	540	152	2978	1019
Southeast	78	89	238	98	323	293	503	667
South Central	90	86	179	163	390	164	250	728
Total East	309	206	639	322	1610	817	4884	2891
Pacific Northwest	2	177	16	365	76	874	10	—1063
Alaska Coast*		8		39	1	166		—127
Cal.-Hawaii		152	14	92	11	338	353	—1475
N. Rocky Mountains		93		84	5	387	13	272
S. Rocky Mountains		46		103	44	177	69	82
Total West	2	476	30	683	137	1942	445	—2311
Total United States	311	682	669	1005	1747	2759	5329	580

Total Hardwoods	= 8056
Total Softwoods	= 5026
Grand Total	= 13,082

* Interior Alaska excluded because of remoteness.

The negative figures in the Net Growth column for western softwoods mean that the big trees are being harvested faster than they are growing. The fact that harvest exceeds growth does not mean there is no wood to burn in the West. Up until a few years ago sawdust was simply burned in wigwam-like contraptions as a way of getting rid of it. These are now largely outlawed and the sawdust piles along the Pacific coast could once again heat houses, as they did until gas and oil became so readily available.

Much of the growth in the East is in trees so twisted and crooked that they will never produce good lumber. The Forest Service estimates one out of every four eastern hardwoods is in the cull class and should be removed, so that growth is shifted into the better trees, just as gardens are improved by thinning. Thus taking wood for fuel from the forests should not compete with the lumber industry at all. On the contrary, it should lead to much greater production of high quality lumber.

Enough for all   The grand total of 13 billion cubic feet in Table I is equivalent to 160 million cords. Since it takes about 5 cords a year to heat the average American house, that is enough wood for 33 million such houses, or almost all of them. Such calculations are meant to do no more than give a concrete example of how much wood is available for fuel in this country. There is, in fact, far more wood available than indicated by the figures in the table, since they do not include cull trees, smaller trees, branches, and deadwood. Nor does the Forest Service count trees along roadsides and between fields, in orchards and backyards. The true annual figure for potential fuelwood may be closer to twice the grand total of 13 billion cubic feet shown in the Table.

The Table also does not show that net growth is increasing year by year as the eastern forests become better stocked. Three-quarters of the total forestland in the United States is in the East where growing conditions are generally good. But much of this land, although classified as forest, is really better described as overgrown pasture. As young, vigorous trees become established on this land, it will produce more and more wood each year.

In the long term it will be necessary to know much more accurately how much solar energy U. S. forests can, with careful management, capture each year. But for our purposes here, it is hardly worthwhile to refine the estimates in Table I. Suffice it to say that the forests of the United States are capturing far more energy today than is being used by man, and that the total amount captured is on the increase.

ENVIRONMENTAL IMPACT   The single, most important fact about the products of combustion of wood is that these would be liberated in the forest by decay anyway and do not, therefore, lead to a net increase in environmental pollution. This is a big assertion needing a good deal of scientific buttressing. As always, the facts are not all in. Nevertheless, we believe the statement to be essentially correct, whether combustion is complete or incomplete.

No CO_2
increase

"The slow smokeless burning of decay," to borrow Robert Frost's phrase, is slow oxidation under the influence of micro-organisms and fungi; combustion is fast oxidation. Complete oxidation of wood is the reverse of photosynthesis, the major products being carbon dioxide, water and energy as heat instead of light. These are the products, whether the oxidation occurs on the forest floor or in the firebox of a stove. Thus burning of wood does not lead to a net increase of atmospheric carbon dioxide, in contrast to coal and oil, since the carbon dioxide would be liberated in the forest by decay anyway.

Incomplete
combustion

However, burning of wood is often incomplete. In home and industrial wood-burners a wide variety of other substances, ranging from the common to the exotic, are produced in addition to carbon dioxide and water. But the point here again is the great similarity between these so-called intermediate products of combustion and those liberated in the forest by decay.[3] Many of the intermediate products are volatile, and, when they are formed in decaying wood, escape into the forest air where they undergo chemical reactions with one another under the influence of sunlight, giving rise to the haze characteristic of forests on hot, still summer days —haze so pronounced in the Smoky Mountains that they take their name from it.

"The slow smokeless burning of decay"—Robert Frost. *Whether oxidation occurs slowly on the forest floor or rapidly in a stove there is no net increase of atmospheric carbon dioxide.*

No one should draw the conclusion that it is harmless to breathe smoke from a wood fire. There is a great deal of chemical analysis to be done before the exact nature of all the intermediates and their fates in the environment are known. Some may turn out to be more hazardous than we now think, but it is perhaps necessary to remind ourselves occasionally that the human race evolved in a world where forest emanations were common.

As might be suspected, there are natural processes for eliminating, as well as producing, these "natural pollutants". Carbon monoxide (yes, carbon monoxide is a natural pollutant from decay of certain plant materials) has been shown to be rendered harmless by microflora of the soil.[4] This is in contrast to the products of nuclear fission, most of which, like strontium-90 and plutonium, are here in megalethal quantities only as a result of human activities, and none of which can be rendered harmless by environmental mechanisms.

SO_2 One pollutant causing a great deal of worry now is sulfur dioxide, which comes from the burning of fossil fuels as well as volcanoes and decaying plant material. It is generally acknowledged to contribute to various lung diseases, and it can inhibit the growth of plants at higher concentrations. In the atmosphere it gives rise to corrosive sulfuric acid that dissolves statues, among other things. But with wood hardly any of this noxious gas is produced. That is not to say that there is no sulfur in trees. On the contrary, it is an element that they cannot live without. But in trees most of the sulfur is in the form of sulfate minerals and not readily converted into sulfur dioxide through combustion.

A reasonable estimate of the sulfur in wood that can be converted to sulfur dioxide by burning is 0.02% by weight.[5] This is to be compared with bituminous coal, more than half of which in this country contains at least 2.5% sulfur that can be converted to the dioxide.[6] Incidentally, sulfur that can be oxidized is the major villain, and the sulfur in coal and oil is largely in the oxidizable form thanks to certain bacteria in the bogs that gave rise to the fossil fuels in the first place.[7]

There are other environmental effects of burning wood which have no direct connection with pollution. Obviously the forest itself is affected by cutting fuelwood. We can cut the way it has been done all too often in the past, depleting the soil of minerals, causing erosion and destroying wildlife. Or we can do it intelligently, in the awareness that this may be our last chance to do it right.

Other effects

PRODUCTIVITY AND ALLOWABLE CUT   Forests change with age the way people do, and forests can be classified as young, middle-aged and old. Very young forests are quite unproductive, when the yardstick of productivity is solar energy captured per acre and later stored as organic matter in leaves, trunk, branches and roots. This follows because the foliage cover in a young forest is poor, and the total photosynthetic rate depends upon the amount of light intercepted by leaves and needles.

On the other extreme, in a forest composed of old trees, the amount of solar energy captured may be high, but most of this goes to simply maintaining the trees, which like people, houses and all organized structures, break down without a constant input of energy. Solar energy used for tree maintenance cannot be used to make wood, and the low productivity of the magnificent Douglas fir and redwood stands in the West is used to justify the heavy cutting of these trees now, the argument being that replacing the big trees with younger, growing ones will lead to more wood in the long run.

Forest productivity   Thorough studies of forest productivity take time, training and money. The ones that have been done indicate that maximum productivity of even-aged stands in the temperate zone occurs when the trees are around 20 years of age.[8] Upon reflection this is hardly surprising, since by then the trees have developed maximum foliage cover, often five or so times greater in area than the ground they occupy, but are still young and vigorous.

Forest productivity decreases in general toward the poles, but there are many isolated examples where this rule is broken, because productivity also depends upon local rainfall, soil type and condition, exposure to sun and man's influence.

Productivity is not just an irrelevant academic concept, but of fundamental importance, since knowing how much organic matter can be produced by solar energy through photosynthesis is essential to answering the question of how many people the earth can support at a reasonably high standard of living. We must ask not only how much organic matter is produced in the forest, but also what fraction of that man may take without upsetting the ecosystem of which he is a part. Answers are beginning to emerge, but they come slowly, not only because trees grow slowly, but also because of the complexity of the forest ecosystem.

At one extreme are some European forests where all wood has been harvested right down to the needles for several centuries. This treatment is less severe than it may seem at first, since almost half the organic matter made in the forest is in roots and leaves or needles, and these parts are usually not harvested. These parts also are richer in minerals than trunk and branches. The intensively managed European forests still appear very productive of both wood and wildlife, although there is some evidence that intensive management may lead to a serious loss of some minerals from the forest.[9] Only now are comprehensive studies being undertaken of the flow of minerals into and out of whole woodlots.[10]

European forests

A related matter (of some controversy among those most knowledgeable in the field) is whether forest productivity can be increased by simple management techniques such as thinning. Clearly lumber production can be enhanced by these measures, but that does not mean that the same is true for total forest productivity. Man has proven over and over that he has the capacity to decrease the productivity of the land—sometimes all the way to zero (as in the American dustbowl and more recently in certain parts of Viet Nam).

It is possible, of course, to raise productivity of crops above natural levels, although not very much and usually at the expense of vast amounts of energy from fossil fuels to make fertilizer and to run all the mechanized equipment common on American farms. The same could be done with forests, but that would only reduce further our fossil-fuel capital, and our objective must be to start living on solar income.

Better forest land in the temperate regions captures and converts into organic matter about one per cent of the incident solar radiation. Man-made solar cells are often ten to 15 per cent efficient, so it is sometimes concluded that we should not use our forests as an energy source, since man's inventions are so much more efficient.

Narrow concept of efficiency

Such a view reflects a very narrow conception of efficiency: It neglects the fact that trees store as well as capture solar energy, and it also fails to take into account all the energy required to produce artificial solar cells—not to mention the pollution from the factories where they are manufactured. We would hope for a durable array of man-made solar cells that would provide food for the woodpecker, a home for the squirrel, pollen for the bee, and improve the soil instead of poisoning it when finished as an energy converter.

But back to your woodlot. In Table II are figures of productivity (now in terms of harvestable wood) as estimated

TABLE II

Potential Forest Production in the United States

Capability Class (cords/year)	Softwoods (millions of acres)	Hardwoods (millions of acres)
1.5 plus	38	16
1 — 1.5	61	56
.63 — 1	93	91
.25 — .63	54	72

by the U. S. Forest Service for the entire 500 million acres in the United States classed as commercial forest.[11] These figures are apt to be low, for the reasons stated above in connection with Table I, but it would not be far wrong to infer from the table that the average *potential* production of harvestable wood on American forestland is on the order of 1 cord/acre/year. (The cord is not a good unit of measure here, but good enough for our purposes.)

These figures give at least an approximate answer to how much land is needed to heat your house over the years. With a well stocked average woodlot you can count on about 1 cord per year from each acre. In the colder parts of the country about 6 cords per winter may be needed, a figure that comes down as insulation and burning efficiencies go up. This implies a woodlot of at least 6 acres, but with only 6 acres you would have to burn some trees suitable for lumber,

An exception to the rule—a manicured even-aged stand of hard-woods.

spend time inefficiently cutting up some very small wood, and also rob the woodpeckers. It would be preferable, therefore, to have 12 acres or more to supply 6 cords of fuelwood annually. These figures can easily be adjusted according to forest productivity and heating requirements in your area.

Some big drafty old houses require as many as 20 cords a winter; on the other hand one well-built 5-room house in Vermont we know of runs comfortably on less than 2 cords a winter.

With experience the numbers can be refined. Whatever the best estimates are, there is no doubt that there is a vast amount of energy in the forest now untapped by man. Our answer to the skeptics is only a partial answer of course. We hope to foster a rational attitude toward the forest as a replacement for delicate sentimentality engendered, perhaps, by awareness of past mistakes. In knowledge of the forest's productivity and its complex ecological relationships lies the key to its use and avoidance of its over-exploitation.

1. The average global temperature has been going down, not up, in the recent past, possibly because of particulate matter in the atmosphere from combustion and volcanoes. *Cleaning our Environment, The Chemical Basis for Action,* Am. Chem. Soc., 1969, p. 34.

2. *Forest Statistics for the United States by State and Region, 1970,* Forest Service, U.S.D.A., 1972.

3. J. A. Hall, *Forest Fuels, Prescribed Fire, and Air Quality,* Pacific Northwest Forest and Range Experiment Station, U.S.D.A., Portland, Ore., 1972.

4. R. E. Inman, R. B. Ingersoll, E. A. Levy, "Soil, a Natural Sink for Carbon Monoxide," *Science,* vol. 172, p. 1729, 1971.

5. Wise (Wise and Jahn, *Wood Chemistry,* ACS Monograph 97, 2nd ed., 1952, p. 651) reports the protein content of sapwood to be about 1 per cent, although in the cambium layer under the bark the protein content can be as high as 30 per cent. According to Meyer and Anderson (*Plant Physiology,* 1939, p. 437) sulfur in plant proteins never exceeds 2 per cent by weight. Therefore a reasonable estimate of oxidizable sulfur in wood is 0.01 x 2 per cent = 0.02 per cent. This compares well with the value of 0.08 per cent reported for mixed bark and wood burned by the Eugene Water and Electric Board in its electric generators (O.D. Brown, *District Heating,* July-August, 1973). There are other possible sources of oxidizable sulfur in wood, but they are relatively unimportant. The low sulfur content in wood has been recognized

for years and that is why wood and charcoal have been used in metallurgical operations where a sulfur-free atmosphere is required.

6. *Environmental Effects of Producing Electric Power,* Joint Committee on Atomic Energy, Part 1, 1969, p. 444.

7. C. J. Pratt, *Scientific American,* May 1970, p. 62.

8. J. D. Ovington, "Quantitative Ecology and the Woodland Ecosystem Concept," *Adv. Ecol. Res.,* Vol. I, 1962, p. 125.

9. Ibid. p. 181.

10. F. H. Bormann & G. E. Likens, "The Nutrient Cycles of an Ecosystem," *Sci. Am.,* Oct., 1970, p. 92.

11. Adapted from the reference in 2 above using 80 cubic feet of wood to the cord.

WOOD TO BURN

FOREST PRODUCTS RESPOND MORE QUICKLY TO the pressures of supply and demand than most other commodities, and this is especially true of fuelwood as evidenced by the "energy crisis" of 1973-74. In northeastern metropolitan areas the price soared to $100 and more per cord. By mid-February the demand at that price had been met and unsold wood was made available at prices far below those of the early winter.

Even in normal times the market is cyclical, with highest prices in March when there is still cold weather ahead and the woodpile is almost gone. The far-sighted buyer will take advantage of the downs in the market and buy in quantity when the price is right. There is little danger of having too much wood. What isn't burned the first winter will keep for the next.

THE CORD   Wood is usually sold by the cord—a stack four feet wide, four feet high, and eight feet long—that is, 128 cubic feet of air and wood. The actual volume of wood is always less, 112 cubic feet for perfect cylinders stacked hexagonally. But for split firewood the actual volume of wood varies between 77 and 96 cubic feet depending on taper, knots, crookedness, and skill of the piler. Back when pulpwood was cut and piled in the woods, cutters developed remarkable skill in piling. The game was to outwit the company scaler and get as little wood as possible into 128 cubic feet.

Often "cord" is applied to a four by eight pile of wood cut twelve, sixteen, or twenty-four inches long. In most states and provinces this is legal so long as it is qualified as a "face cord". Consumer protection laws have not yet been extended to fuelwood, and it is up to the buyer to find out just how much wood he buys in *stove cords, pick-up cords* and *fireplace cords*. The definitions are vague and vary from place to place. One state used to define a cord as the product of a four by four by eight pile. Purchasers were disappointed because their sixteen or twenty-four inch sticks occupied less than 128 cubic feet when piled at home. But they may not have been cheated, since cutting to shorter lengths reduces crookedness and allows closer packing.

Variety of "cords"

A simple device can be constructed at home to help estimate the amount of solid wood in a pile. Make a grid two or three feet square from a wooden frame and strings or wires so that there are 100 intersections. Hang the grid on the woodpile and if 35 of the intersections miss wood (65 must hit) 65 per cent of the pile is solid wood, that is, 83 cubic feet of wood to the cord. In industry the same thing is done with a camera and a transparent dot grid.

CHOICE OF FUELWOOD   The potential energy of a cord depends on the weight of actual wood in it, regardless of species. The logical way to sell wood would be by weight if the moisture in it were not so variable. Half the weight of freshly cut (green) wood may be due to water. After thorough drying (seasoning) under ordinary outdoor conditions the weight of absorbed water is still about 20 per cent of the weight of bone-dry wood. For the moment we will assume we are dealing with air-dried (20 per cent moisture) wood.

The densest fuelwood is the best. In Table III species are arranged according to density with the densest at the top of each column. All the woods in the left column make excellent fuel, those in the middle are OK, and those on the right can be used in a pinch.   *Densest wood is best*

Inspection of the table shows that the woods used most extensively in construction are by and large in the righthand column. Carpenters prefer to work with the softer woods. In the lefthand column only the oaks, black birch and longleaf pine are in much demand for lumber and veneer; thus there is a fortuitous natural division which precludes cutthroat

TABLE III

Densities of Various North American Woods

Hardwoods

High	Medium	Low
LIVE OAKS	SUGAR MAPLE	RED ALDER
EUCALYPTUS	AMERICAN BEECH	LARGE TOOTH
HOP HORNBEAM	HONEY LOCUST	ASPEN
DOGWOOD	YELLOW BIRCH	BASSWOOD
HICKORY	WHITE ASH	CHESTNUT
SHADBUSH	ELM	CATALPA
PERSIMMON	BLACK GUM	BLACK WILLOW
WHITE OAK	RED MAPLE	BOX ELDER
BLACK BIRCH	BLACK WALNUT	TULIP POPLAR
BLACK LOCUST	PAPER BIRCH	BUTTERNUT
APPLE	RED GUM	QUAKING ASPEN
BLUE BEECH	CHERRY	COTTONWOOD
CRABS	HOLLY	WILLOW
RED OAK	GREY BIRCH	BALSAM POPLAR
	SYCAMORE	
	OREGON ASH	
	SASSAFRAS	
	MAGNOLIA	

Softwoods

High	Medium	Low
SLASH PINE	YEW	PONDEROSA PINE
POND PINE	TAMARACK	RED FIR
WESTERN LARCH	NUT PINES	NOBLE FIR
LONGLEAF PINE	(PINYON)	BLACK SPRUCE
	SHORTLEAF PINE	BALD CYPRESS
	JUNIPERS	REDWOOD
	LOBLOLLY PINE	HEMLOCKS
	DOUGLAS FIR	SITKA SPRUCE
	PITCH PINE	YELLOW CEDAR
	RED CEDAR	WHITE SPRUCE
	NORWAY PINE	WHITE PINE
		BALSAM FIR
		WESTERN RED
		CEDAR
		SUGAR PINE

competition between cutters of fuelwood and timber.

The order in Table III is only approximate, since density will vary within each species. In general wood grown under favorable conditions is denser than slower growing wood of the same species. There are cases of beech more dense than sugar maple and cherry more dense than elm, but you won't find American elm denser than hickory.

Surprising, perhaps, is the fact that some so-called softwoods are very dense and every bit as good as oak for fuel. But since the softwoods tend to grow away from major population centers most people are unacquainted with those that do make good fuel, although the densest pines are found near Jacksonville and Miami. The only major cities in North America having no reasonably dense fuelwood within hauling distance are Edmonton, Calgary, Denver, Tucson and Phoenix. *Some softwoods are good fuel*

The terms *hardwood* and *softwood* are in fact misnomers used as common synonyms for the more formidable terms Angiosperms and Gymnosperms, which are taxonomic labels based on reproductive differences. There are also differences in cell structure between the two kinds of trees. Softwoods are often more resinous too, a fact giving them a slight edge in fuel value per pound of dry wood.

COMPARISON OF WOOD AND OIL PRICES There are considerations other than price that affect choice of fuels, such as guaranteed availability, ease of handling, and kind

TABLE IV

Fuel Values of Some Common Woods

	Average Density (lb./cord; 20% moisture)	Fuel Value/Cord (BTUs)	Price/Cord Equivalent to Oil at 41¢/gallon*
Shagbark Hickory	4400	30.8 million	$69
White Oak	4400	30.8	69
Sugar Maple	4100	29.7	66
American Beech	4000	28.0	63
Red Oak	3900	27.3	61
Yellow Birch	3800	26.6	59
White Ash	3700	25.9	58
American Elm	3400	23.8	54
Red Maple	3400	23.8	54
Paper Birch	3400	23.8	54
Black Cherry	3300	23.1	51
Douglas Fir	2900	21.4	48
Eastern White Pine	2200	15.8	35

* Assumed efficiencies: wood stove, 50%; oil furnace, 65%.[1]

and cost of burning equipment required. But it is useful to be able to compare the price of wood with oil BTU for BTU. The results are presented in Table IV.

The figures in the table were established as follows: the densities are averages of data found in various technical sources. Any actual density measurement could easily be different from the ones in Table IV by 15 per cent. In fact, close inspection will show minor disagreements between Tables III and IV.

The energy liberated on burning one pound of bone-dry wood completely is called its fuel value—about 8600 BTUs. But air-dried wood is around 20 per cent water by weight, and the heat liberated on burning a pound of air-dried wood is therefore less—about 7000 BTUs. The third column is obtained from the second by multiplying by 7000 for the hardwoods and by 7360 for Douglas fir and 7200 for white pine to take into account the inflammable resins in the latter two. Thus the figures in the third column represent maximum heating effect from a cord of wood and must be modified by an efficiency factor to estimate the actual amount of heat transferred to the house. The best wood stoves are about 50 per cent efficient under household conditions (see Chapter III), and to be realistic, all the figures in the third column should be halved to find actual heating effect.[2]

Oil furnaces are about 65 per cent efficient under household conditions. Since the fuel value of one gallon of heating oil is 140,000 BTUs, the heating effect from one gallon is 91,000 BTUs. At 41¢ per gallon that amounts to 45¢ per thousand useful BTUs. At the same price, the 14 million useful BTUs from a cord of American beech would cost $63. Thus beech at anything less than $63 a cord is cheaper than oil at 41¢ a gallon. All the figures in the fourth column have been calculated similarly. Should the price of oil change, new figures for that column can be calculated by simple proportions.

The density column is also worth looking at. A cord of

good beech, even after drying, weighs about 2 tons. This should make one suspicious of any alleged cord delivered in a ½- or ¾-ton pickup truck.

DETERMINING DRYNESS   It is to the hauler's advantage to deliver dry wood, since absorbed moisture means extra weight on the springs and more trips per cord. Still, if you buy wood that is advertized as dry, you want to be able to verify it easily. People familiar with firewood simply know when it is dry—by appearance (are there cracks?), sound (when two sticks are hit together do you hear the high-pitched ring of the bowling alley or a low-pitched thud?), smell, weight; if in doubt, the safest thing is to split a sample log and try burning the sticks.

Effect of water   Water in wood does not lower the fuel value of a cord; the amount of actual wood and consequently the heat of combustion does not depend on the amount of absorbed water. But water does reduce the overall heating efficiency, because it takes energy to vaporize water and heat it to the temperature of the flue gases. This energy loss in itself is not very significant. The problem with wet wood is that its cooling effect is often just enough to prevent complete combustion. Therefore, burn green wood on a hot fire if you have to burn it at all. The way to keep wet wood burning is to split it up into small sticks.

Having dry wood can mean the difference between seren-

The traditional way was to cut to four or five foot lengths in the woods and to finish cutting with the cord wood saw, usually run on tractor power.

ity and an ulcer. If no dry wood is available, ash is the pre-
ferred green wood because its moisture content is relatively
low on the stump. No doubt that's the reason for its good
reputation, since its density is not all that high. According to
an anonymous English poet:

Beechwood fires are bright and clear
If the logs are kept a year.
Chestnut only good, they say,
If for long 'tis laid away.
But ash new or ash old
Is fit for queen with crown of gold.

Birch and fir logs burn too fast,
Blaze up bright and do not last.
It is by the Irish said
Hawthorn bakes the sweetest bread.
Elm wood burns like churchyard mold,.
E'en the very flames are cold.
But ash green or ash brown
Is fit for queen with golden crown.

Poplar gives a bitter smoke,
Fills your eyes and makes you choke.
Apple wood will scent your room
With an incense like perfume.
Oaken logs, if dry and old,
Keep away the winter's cold.
But ash wet or ash dry
A king shall warm his slippers by.

WHERE TO FIND WOOD   For many people, working
up the winter's wood is good exercise and relaxation. Opportunities exist to enjoy it even if you don't own a woodlot.
Some state forests have been opened to fuelwood cutters for
nothing or next to nothing. Just drive up, cut your wood and
haul it away. The trees to cut are usually marked in advance
by a forester.

Urban dwellers may find the town dump a rich source of
wood and closer to home. Big logs take up much valuable
space as land fill and might as well keep someone warm. This
suggestion may be resisted by city fathers infected with the
bureaucratic mind. But persist. It really is quite feasible to
dump logs off to the side for scavengers who perform a civic
good by disposing of them in the stove or fireplace.

Hardwood tops left in the woods after logging operations
make excellent firewood if not left long enough to rot. The
owner may be glad to have you cut them up, because dry
tops are a fire hazard in time of drought.

*Dry tops
fire
hazard*

Some woodland owners, especially those in the Tree Farm
Program, know the value of thinning, and they may be re-
ceptive to a suggestion of exchanging their wood for your
labor. The county forester can often help likely parties get in
touch with one another.

WOODLAND IMPROVEMENT   In the West there is a
huge quantity of mill wastes to be used as fuel. In the East

most fuelwood will have to come from forests that are desperately in need of improvement work if they are ever to produce high quality wood products at the rate they are capable of. In almost all cases fuelwood should be a secondary product and a valuable tool in promoting growth of good saw and veneer logs, although at $100/cord, tall straight sound trees bring a higher profit as sticks for the fireplace.

Thinning Much of the eastern forest has been lumbered several times, and each time the best has been taken and the worst left. This practice has altered the composition drastically in favor of species of less economic value and individual trees of unmarketable quality. Many eastern hardwoods are growing in clumps of four or five, all having sprouted from the same stump and all are bent and crooked as a result of growing toward the light and away from one another.

The object of removing the crooked, the moribund and the economically unimportant is to shift growth into the straight, the healthy and the economically important trees. Choosing the ones to cut is fairly easy, but there are some pitfalls. Making a few mistakes is nothing to worry about though, since in all probability you will do more good than harm, so bad is the condition of the eastern woodlands.

Pointer 1 · How To Recognize Sawlogs. What is an acceptable sawlog varies with the species and the products being manufactured, but generally sawlogs are straight and

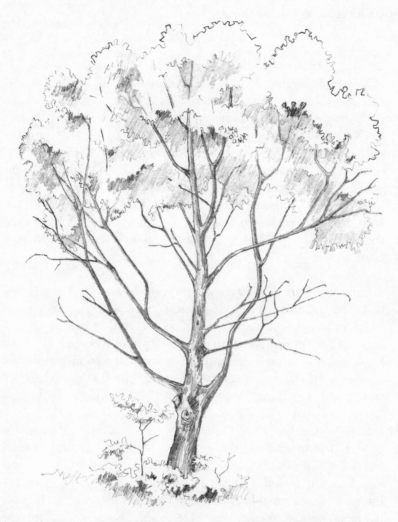

The "wolf" tree has many limbs and an excessively large crown. It may contain a short low quality sawlog, but should be eliminated because it grows at the expense of potential crop trees.

at least eight feet long with a diameter of at least eight inches for hardwoods and six inches for softwoods. There are certain species that are reasonably safe bets to favor for sawtimber, although there are, of course, exceptions depending on local conditions. The list of desirable hardwood species in continuous demand is: red and white oak; yellow, black and white (paper) birch; sugar maple; red gum; ash; basswood; tulip poplar; cherry; walnut. A similar generalization for softwoods is harder to make, except that in regions where they grow the prevailing softwood should be favored over hardwoods.

Pointer 2 · How To Recognize Wolf Trees.   A wolf tree is a large, crooked tree with many limbs and an excessively large crown taking up a lot of space and growing at the expense of potential crop trees. It may contain a short low quality sawlog, but should be eliminated in any case. Inexperienced chain saw operators, who should stick to smaller trees until skilled, can accomplish this by girdling.

Pitfall 1 · Cutting The Undergrowth.   For far too many owners the immediate desire is to clean up the underbrush to make the woods look parklike and easier to walk and ski through. But the brush is the next crop of trees in infancy, it takes an inordinate amount of labor to cut it, and it has its own ecological role. Deer, for instance, can browse only as high as their necks will let them.

Pitfall 2 · Cutting Too Many Small Trees.   Fuelwood
can be cut from any tree, but it takes about two hundred
three-inch trees to get a cord, and if you cut too many
of them you are going to be disappointed in the time necessary to make up your woodpile. Furthermore, the competition for light in a dense stand of young trees promotes the
growth of tall, straight, knot-free trees.

Pitfall 3 · Thinning Too Heavily.   Trees protect one another from the wind. Big open spaces allow the wind to
get in among the trees and throw over the shallow-rooted
ones. Too much sun all of a sudden can put a physiologi-
cal strain on species that tolerate the shadiness of the
understory well when young—beech and sugar maple for
example. Therefore, thinning should be done in stages, rather
than in one vain attempt to make a model forest overnight.

HAULING   Before you cut a single tree, better figure
out how to get the tree home, and this is something not mentioned in the chain saw manual. Transportation of wood is
the most costly step in the whole process. Many methods of
hauling have been used, including human backs, waterways,
horses, mules, oxen, elephants, crawler tractors, articulated
skidders, chutes, flumes, railroads, trucks, and most recently
helicopters and balloons. On this continent more of it has
been transported by four-footed animals than by any other
method.

Four feet go where tires can't, and do less damage.

Whenever possible the step of stacking in the woods is to be avoided. The most efficient sequence is cut, load, haul and pile the wood close to the house. This also lessens the likelihood of theft. There may be good reasons, however, for stacking in the woods: 1) if the condition of the forest floor is such that a vehicle or team cannot maneuver, and 2) if the hauling distance is very long, in which case stacking and drying are done first to reduce the wood's weight and therefore the number of trips.

As a general rule the logs taken out of the woods should be large enough to fully utilize the power available. That may mean tree length pieces, which come out of rough woods easier if the front end is raised. Power for this can be supplied by two-wheel-drive farm tractors (suitable for relatively smooth and dry woodlots), four-wheel-drive vehicles (suitable for somewhat rougher conditions), horses, mules, or oxen (suitable for still rougher conditions).

Hauling power

Most horses and mules today have not had the training of the old time faithful skid animals. But they have advantages over some of the other sources of power in that they have brains, don't have to be steered, and have built-in rear view vision enabling them to see what they are pulling and anticipate difficulties. The affluent Sixties have increased the horse population in many parts of semi-rural America. Arabians, Quarter horses and Morgans should not be ruled out even though they were originally trained for other tasks.

When logging was primarily dependent on animal power,

forest products were seldom hauled uphill, and the old logging roads are still likely to be best for getting wood out.
However, these old roads have not always stood the ravages
of time, and it may be expensive and environmentally harmful to restore them. With more power, uphill skidding is possible and may cause less erosion.

FELLING AND BUCKING   You could drag out your
ancestors' buck or two-man saws and sharpen them up, but

Hand saws   the Swedish bow saw and modern chain saws *do* make the
work much easier. The former because of the thinness of the
blade, made possible by putting good Swedish charcoal (no
sulfur!) steel under tension. This means less sawdust and
consequently less work. The bow saw is good for pruning as
well as felling and bucking, but it simply is not suited to felling trees in the 20-inch class. For $5 you are in business and
$2 buys a new blade when the original can no longer be
sharpened.

Chain saws   Chain saws require frequent sharpening and much more
maintenance than a bow saw. As a rule of thumb, they are
justifiable if you will be cutting at least 2 cords a year. They
appeared in the woods in the mid-Forties and have been con-
sistently improved and lightened since then. For the most
part the latest models weigh between six and fifteen pounds.
Of course the lightest ones are the easiest to use, and they
perform acceptably on small trees. In general the more wood

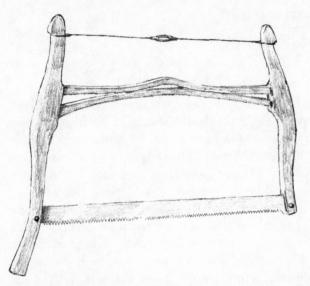

The bucksaw has cut many American trees into stove-length pieces. Before the turnbuckle, tension was provided by a rawhide thong tightened by twisting. A loose blade makes too wide a cut and too much work.

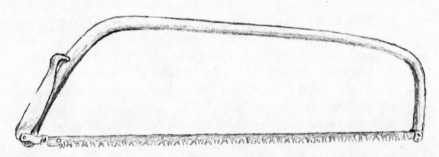

The Swedish bowsaw has largely replaced the old-fashioned bucksaw, because its thinner blade and raker teeth make the work easier. The teeth are hardened by a special process and stay sharp longer.

you expect to cut, the bigger the chain saw you should buy.

If you live in an area of frequent power failures and already own a portable generator, you might consider an electric saw. The electric saw plus generator costs more than a gasoline saw, but less than a gasoline saw and generator. Besides, electric saws are quieter and have greater overall efficiency when run on house current (because the power plant is more efficient than either the generator or the gasoline saw). The energy gain of the gasoline chain saw is about 500, that is, 1 BTU from burning gasoline cuts about 500 BTUs worth of wood.

Energy gain with chain saw

Chain saw manufacturers have been vying with one another to reduce the noise of their saws, but with little success. You should consider the pros and cons of ear plugs. When the chain saw is running you can't hear anything, and over long periods the noise does impair one's hearing of the higher pitches. If you are young and want to enjoy fine music in later life, use ear plugs, but remember that if you are not working alone, you won't hear anything your companions say, even when the saw is not going.

Incidentally, they run nicely on unleaded gas.

The chain saw manual makes felling sound simple, and it really is if all the forces are properly evaluated. A straight, well-balanced tree can be felled in any direction. First undercut it in the direction you want it to go—preferably away from trees that will make good lumber in a few years. The undercut is a wedge-shaped notch made with two cuts about

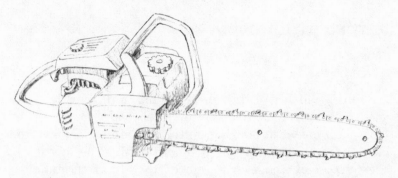

The chain saw makes heating with wood possible for many who have only weekends for working up the woodpile. It can, of course, do great harm. The fact that the accident rate with chain saws is higher among professionals than amateur woodcutters suggests that carelessness bred by familiarity must be constantly guarded against.

one-third of the way through the trunk. The Humbolt under-cut, in which the slanting cut is made below the first, is best if the butt is going to be made into a sawlog, because it saves valuable wood for lumber. But for fuelwood the slanting cut may be above the first cut, since it's easier to do.

The felling cut is made horizontally from the opposite side of the tree slightly above the undercut. Within an inch or two of the undercut, depending on the diameter of the tree, the felling cut is stopped to leave a hinge. If the tree does not fall of its own accord, a felling wedge is inserted and the tree is wedged over.

Unfortunately not all trees are straight and evenly weighted, especially cull trees. If a tree leans the way you want to fell it, the undercut must be made deeper, since otherwise there

Avoiding
the pinched
bar

are forces which will split the butt end, a disaster for saw-logs and a dangerous time-saver for fuelwood.

When it comes to bucking up the tree after it is down the biggest nuisance and waste of time is getting the saw stuck. The purpose of wedges is to remedy that, but a careful evaluation of the forces can avoid having to use them. The top of your downed tree is either under tension or compression: tension if it is suspended free and compression otherwise. When it is under tension there is no danger of the saw getting stuck, but the weight of the top end tends to split the log before a downward cut is completed. To prevent this, cut up from underneath, but not far enough to get the saw stuck; then finish with a cut from the upper side to meet the under-cut. If the top is under compression, reverse the procedure by cutting down first. If you get the saw stuck, you will have to resort to the wedge, but it is easier to drive the wedge from the top down, so if you must get the saw stuck, get it stuck in a top cut. Wedges for this purpose are made of wood, magnesium or plastic, since a new chain costs over $20. If the saw gets stuck in a horizontal felling cut, it is safest to remove the motor from the bar and chain before trying to dislodge them. This lessens the chance of bending the bar.

After your tree is down take your time and look it over carefully to see which parts are under tension and which under compression. You will find that there is as a rule less saw binding if you start at the top and work toward the butt end.

Sawlogs and pulpwood must be carefully measured, but fuelwood can usually be cut accurately enough by eye or by comparison with the length of your saw or bar.

If your tree did not fall all the way to the ground, you *Hung-up* have what is called a hung-up tree. Beavers frequently get *tree* their trees hung up. They just think "oh well" and go try another tree. But to man a hung-up tree is a bit of a disgrace, a sign of ineptitude. Some cutters have gone about getting it down by cutting the tree in which the first was hung up. They are not all alive today.

Another method is to climb the hung-up tree and try to shake it down, but check to make sure your hospitalization coverage is up to date before attempting this. A third method is to drop another tree on the first to dislodge it. The result is usually two hung-up trees. The beaver may know something we don't.

If one ignores the tree, the wind may bring it down in a few days. If that doesn't work, there are three possibilities left. If you have a peavey and the tree is not too big, you *Peavey* may be able to roll it away from whatever is holding it. Keep your eye on the tree and your footing secure, because you can't always anticipate what the butt is going to do. If that fails, the butt will have to be moved. The peavey or crow bar can be used as a lever to lift and work it backward if the tree is not too large. As a last resort you will have to go get more power. When tired, quit for the day; the tree will wait.

Stumps should usually be cut as low as possible, but with

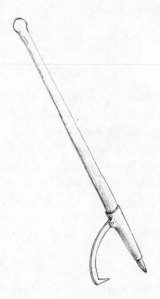

The peavey is a useful tool for dislodging hung-up trees, rolling logs, and even carrying logs if two are used as handles.

the chain saw it is possible to cut sawlogs too low. A flare on the end makes cross-grained lumber and veneer. If the tree has evidence of having metal in it (barbed wire, nails, sap spouts) cut above these sawtooth ruiners. Butts with excessive rot are unpredictable in felling. It's safer to cut above the most rotten part. Otherwise low stumps are desirable because they are more apt to produce healthy sprouts for the next generation of trees and because they are easier on mechanical equipment. A foot of light snow is not much of a hindrance to a four-wheel-drive vehicle, but a ten inch stump hidden under the snow brings the vehicle to an abrupt halt.

SPLITTING   Some woods must be split, paper birch for example, since its bark is so waterproof that it will rot before drying if left unsplit. But for all species splitting speeds drying. It is also good exercise and a harmless way to vent aggressive tendencies that might get you into trouble if not shunted into this productive enterprise. Some woods have a reputation for being tough splitters. We think of elm, black gum (pepperidge), and grey birch. Rock maple is aptly named. Usually the lighter woods split easier than the heavy ones, but straightness of grain and absence of large knots are the most important factors, and these depend not only on species but also on growing conditions. The easiest logs to split are often also the best for lumber, and there is a temptation, to be resisted, to make firewood out of potential lumber.

Split between the knots unless you can bisect them perfectly. Partially dry wood will have cracks on the ends. Split along these cracks and save some effort. Most pieces split easier from the butt toward the top, but don't pass up good opportunities wherever you find them. Frozen wood often splits easier than unfrozen.

Wood splitting tools come in all sizes and shapes, from *Splitting* huge power wedges to Boy Scout hatchets. The former will *tools* reduce a giant redwood to highway dimensions, and the latter is excellent if your wife complains that the kindling is too large. If your prized old maple or elm has to be removed, mechanized splitters can be rented, but they are tools of the professional as a rule. The old black powder wedges too often became rockets and should be dismissed as a possibility. Remember, there are plenty of logs in the forest, it won't hurt to leave a few unsplit. Or you can cheat with a chain saw. It was not designed for ripping a log end to end, but it can do it.

Axes can be used for splitting, but skill is required. Furthermore, the axe should be fatter than for felling and limbing. The way they come from the hardware store is about right for splitting. But for most people two wedges (the second in case the first gets buried in the log without splitting it) and a splitting hammer are the tools. A splitting hammer has a six to twelve pound head similar to a sledge hammer except that one end is in the form of a blunt wedge for administering the *coup de grace*. Despite the weight of the hammer, splitting need not be strenuous. The hammer is heavy enough to do the work. All it needs is direction. Keep your eye on the wedge. Too much violence just breaks the hammer handle.

A good hammer

With frozen wood there is a tendency for the wedge to pop out before it really gets started. The remedy is to sharpen the wedge and then to tap lightly until it takes hold. If that fails, the chain saw can be used to make a small notch to get the wedge started.

SEASONING   Drying takes time, but splitting, sensible stacking, and favorable weather can shorten the process. In

A splitting hammer and two wedges are absolutely necessary for the serious woodsplitter.

most live trees wood has a high moisture content, in the light outer sapwood frequently over 100% in relation to bone-dry wood. Unless it rots first, wood will reach a moisture content of 12-18 per cent depending on local climate. When a forest tree dies there are many organisms ready to recycle that tree back to the earth and air. We want to recycle it in a different way. In a living tree most decay is in the dark heartwood, since the sapwood is too moist. But once the sapwood begins to lose moisture, decay sets in and continues until the wood gets too dry for the decomposers.

Our task is to get the moisture below 20 per cent as soon as possible and air is our tool. Get the wood up off the ground and piled on rocks or unwanted logs so that air can circulate through it as soon as possible, with one exception. When in leaf, trees may be cut and left for a few weeks before bucking. Until the leaves dry up the tree will continue to lose water through them.

Stacking for quick drying

Drying is fastest when the wood is "penned" or "chimneyed", *i.e.* two sticks, then two at right angles and so on up. Piling in the more conventional way allows less circulation of air around the sticks and requires supports at either end. If these are trees, their swaying with the wind sometimes topples the pile and bruises the trees in any case. A combination of a conventional pile between two pens works well.

Generally the best drying time is in the windy spring months before the hardwoods leaf out to shade the forest floor. Spring-cut wood can be burned the following winter. However, people who are really on top of it dry the wood out of doors the first summer and in the barn the next. They then burn, presumably with great contentment, exquisitely dry wood in the second winter.

A woodshed is not really necessary, but it is prudent to have some dry wood under cover at all times. Polyethylene covers, old planks and metal sheets all keep off snow and ice without raising the taxes. Half a cord or so tucked away somewhere in the house is good insurance against occasional sieges of intensely inclement weather.

The fifteen minutes you take to make the sawbuck is soon repaid in effort and headaches saved.

1. C. M. Summers, "The Conversion of Energy," *Scientific American,* Sept. 1971, p. 151.

2. The terminology must be watched closely, since usage varies. Here "fuel value" is the same as "heat of combustion," *i.e.,* the heat liberated when a specified quantity of wood is burned completely with wood, oxygen and products all at the same temperature. Sometimes one sees figures for the *fuel value, available heat* or *heat content* of wood drastically lower than those in Table IV. Such numbers are obtained by making a deduction to account for heat carried away by flue gases on the basis of certain, often unstated, assumptions. It is a serious error to compare such numbers with the fuel value of oil (140,000 BTU/gallon), since this is a comparison of non-comparables that seriously underestimates the true value of wood as fuel.

STOVES
AND OTHER
WOOD-BURNERS

To BURN WOOD IS EASY, BUT TO BURN IT EFFI-ciently is another matter. Unfortunately, about half the heat value of fuelwood goes up the chimney, even with today's best stoves. Perhaps one reason for this inefficiency is the small demand for better wood stoves and furnaces during the last century, but a more fundamental reason is that wood is an unconcentrated fuel of irregular shape and size.

To burn wood efficiently is especially difficult because half its fuel value is in "volatiles"—combustible gases given off when wood gets hot. The other half of wood's fuel value is in the carbonized residue left after all the volatiles have distilled away. Thus the efficient wood-burner must be an efficient gas-burner and an efficient solid-burner simultaneously. It is easier to achieve one or the other than both in the same fire-box.

Perhaps a good way to gain an appreciation of wood stove design is to back up a bit. One of the earliest human uses of wood doubtless was as fuel for cooking. At first this was probably done in the open, but at some point the fire was moved indoors where it provided a modicum of bodily comfort as well. Air heated by the fire and laden with smoke went out through a hole in the roof and was replaced by cooler air coming in through doors and other openings.

The inhabitants of these primitive dwellings must have breathed a good deal of smoke, until someone discovered that putting a stack over the roof hole improved the draft and made the atmosphere inside more bearable. Gradually the fireplace and its associated chimney evolved, followed by stoves, as wood scarcity demanded and technology permitted.

The real "Franklin"

In 1740 the threat of a fuelwood shortage around Philadelphia moved Benjamin Franklin to design his "Pennsylvanian Fire-place." In Franklin's own words: *By the help of this saving invention our wood may grow as fast as we consume it, and our posterity may warm themselves at a moderate rate, without being obliged to fetch their fuel over the Atlantic.*[1]

By his own estimate the ordinary fireplaces of his day were at best 17 per cent efficient. They were, and are, so bad in this respect that, again according to Franklin, supplying and tending them required one man's full time on the larger farms near Philadelphia.[2] After considering several possible designs, he finally decided on the one in the next illustration below. Clearly the Pennsylvanian fireplace bears little resemblance to today's "Franklin" stove, a use of his name that would cause Ben to shudder.

Being culturally English, Franklin wanted to view the fire, but he also realized that a large opening in front allowed too much heated air to go up the chimney without contributing to combustion ("blowing up the fire"). Thus he provided a shutter sliding in grooves to limit the draft to what was needed. He thereby also avoided a bad conscience, since toleration of inefficiency was to him a moral failing.

He directed that the stove be luted (*i.e.* joints sealed) to *"Air-tight"* eliminate unplanned drafts. The desirability of doing this became generally appreciated in 1836 when Isaac Orr of Washington, D.C. patented his "air-tight" stove. Thereafter, airtight became a generic term for a class of stoves made from sheet iron having tight joints and controlled drafts. Today's best stoves are all airtights.

An "air-box", a forerunner of today's heat-o-later was also built into the Pennsylvanian fireplace. Fresh air was drawn up from the cellar and into the box where it followed a long, winding path before exiting at the top on both sides. Warm currents from the air-box were directed at the usually chilly corners of the room flanking the fireplace. To keep the air-box as hot as possible, Franklin channeled the flames and hot gases up and over the box. Since a downward flow of hot gases is unnatural, his stove must have required a good chimney, but he knew how to build those too. His essay "On the

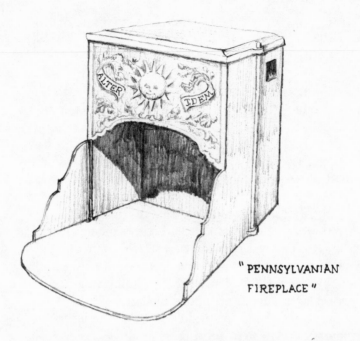

"PENNSYLVANIAN
FIREPLACE"

"In common chimneys, the strongest heat from the fire, which is upwards, goes directly up the chimney, and is lost; and there is such a strong draft into the chimney, that not only the upright heat, but also the back, sides, and downward heats are carried up the chimney by that draft of air; and the warmth given before the fire, by the rays that strike out towards the room, is continually driven back, crowded into the chimney, and carried up by the same draft of air. But here the upright heat strikes and heats the top plate, which warms the air above it, and that comes into the room. The heat likewise, which the fire communicates to the sides, back, bottom, and air-box, is all brought into the room; for you will find a constant current of warm air coming out of the chimney corner into the room."—Benjamin Franklin

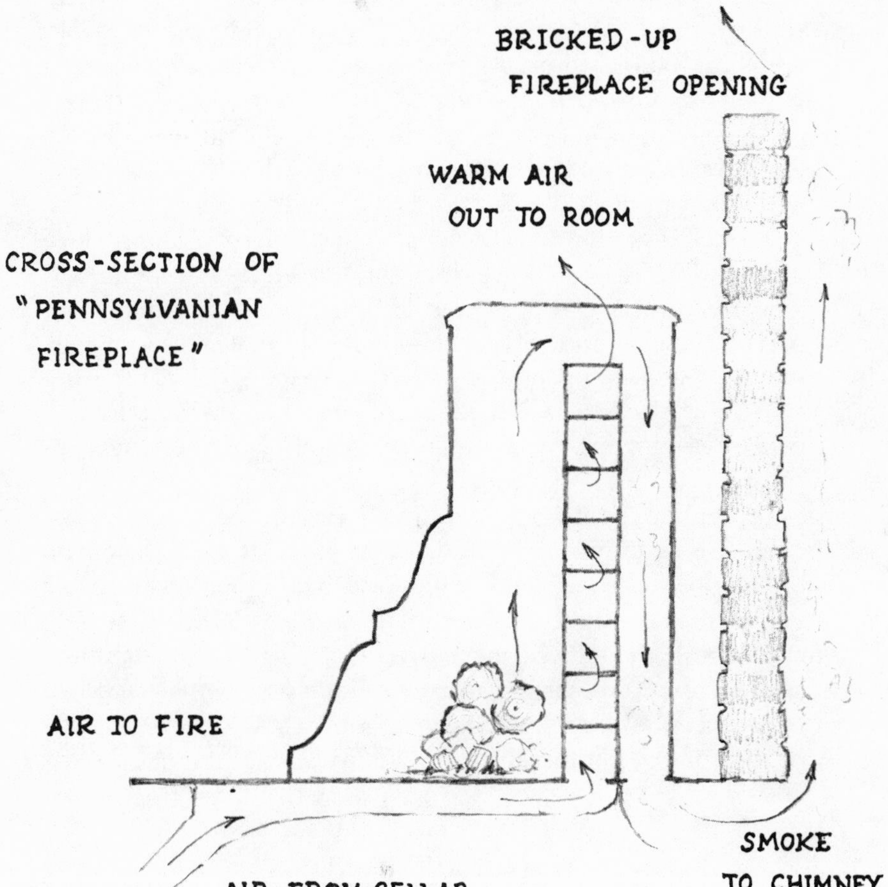

BRICKED-UP
FIREPLACE OPENING

WARM AIR
OUT TO ROOM

CROSS-SECTION OF
"PENNSYLVANIAN
FIREPLACE"

AIR TO FIRE

AIR FROM CELLAR

SMOKE
TO CHIMNEY

Causes and Cure of Smoky Chimneys" still makes worthwhile reading.

Franklin comments on the fuel saved by the Pennsylvanian fireplace: "People who have used these fireplaces differ much in their accounts of the wood saved by them. Some say five-sixths, others three-fourths, and others much less . . . My common room, I know, is made twice as warm as it used to be, with a quarter of the wood I formerly consumed there."

The problem not solved by Franklin in 1740 was how to ensure complete combustion of the volatiles. This is hardly surprising in view of the fact that Priestley had not yet discovered oxygen and Lavoisier's analysis of the chemistry of combustion was still 40 years in the future. But Franklin was well aware of the energy wasted when smoke was not completely burned, and rose to the challenge in 1771 by inventing his "smoke-consuming" stove based on downdraft design. This stove was intended for coal, but instructions for constructing a firebox suitable for wood also were thoughtfully given.

"Smoke-consuming" stove

Bituminous coal gives rise to volatiles as does wood. In an open fire or an ordinary updraft stove fresh fuel placed on top of glowing coals will first lose water and then combustible volatiles as the fuel gets hotter. It is the volatiles that give rise to the long flame from wood, and, if not completely burned, they are carried up the chimney as smoke. Even a large excess of oxygen will not ensure their complete combustion if the temperature in the firebox falls much below 1000°F.

In an updraft stove volatiles are swept up away from the glowing coals, the hottest part of the fire. If the draft is great enough, they go up and out into the open atmosphere; but if the draft is low, the wood wet, and the top of the chimney cool, some are deposited on the inside surfaces of the chimney as so-called creosote.* The obvious solution is to reverse the direction of the draft so that volatiles are carried downward and burned completely in the heat of the coals.

Downdraft design

Theory is one thing, implementation another. Franklin successfully operated the coal version of his downdraft stove for three winters in England and later also in America. But operation was difficult, and unpleasant back-puffing occurred unless the chimney was hot and drawing well. In fact, back-puffing was so troublesome that Franklin recommended that "ignorant servants" not be permitted to tend the stove, since they invariably allowed smoke into the room. He saw this stove as especially suitable for men of letters who, spending much time in their chambers, would be on hand to tend the stove as needed. The trick was to open the draft wide a few minutes before refueling so that the chimney got hot and was drawing maximally when fresh fuel was added from above. In this way all back currents could be avoided, and the smoke would go down through the coals to be burned. With modern stoves that back-puff the trick still is to get the chimney hot just before reloading.

---

* *Creosote used as a wood preservative is made from the distillation of coal.*

SMOKE-CONSUMING STOVE

"The effect of this machine, well managed, is to burn not only the coals, but all the smoke of the coals, so that while the fire is burning, if you go out and observe the top of your chimney, you will see no smoke issuing, nor any thing but clear warm air, which as usual makes the bodies seen through it appear waving.

But let none imagine from this, that it may be a cure for bad or smoky chimneys, much less, that, as it burns the smoke, it may be used in a room that has no chimney. It is by the help of a good chimney, the higher the better, that it produces its effect."

—Benjamin Franklin

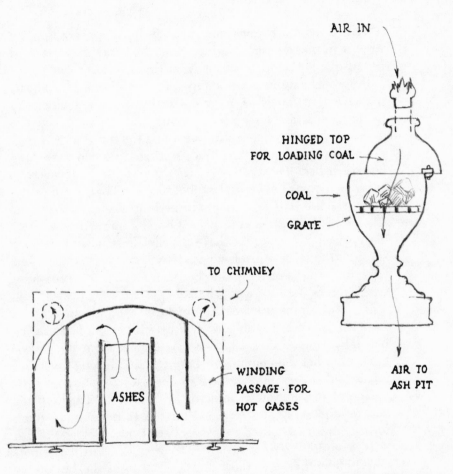

AIR IN

HINGED TOP
FOR LOADING COAL

COAL →

GRATE →

AIR TO
ASH PIT

CROSS-SECTION

TO CHIMNEY

WINDING
PASSAGE FOR
HOT GASES

ASHES

TOP VIEW OF BASE

True downdraft stoves and furnaces have appeared on the American market from time to time, but none has survived because of the same difficulties that Franklin experienced.

Before leaving Franklin temporarily, his least-known heating invention should be mentioned, if only as a challenge to modern experimenters. *Revolving grate* The revolving grate was conceived of as a simplified smoke-consuming stove for the common people who would have difficulty operating the downdraft stove just described. The grate was strictly an updraft device, but consumed smoke nevertheless, because the coals were at the top of the fire. This was accomplished by adding fresh fuel at the top of the grate and turning it one half a revolution after closing it. Volatiles from the fresh fuel thus had to pass up through the layer of coals where they burned. Franklin liked the round shape of the grate, because for him it represented "the Greater Giver of warmth to our system".

None of Franklin's heating inventions lasted in original form. Since he did not believe in profiting unduly from his natural talents—(after all, didn't he benefit from the inventions of others?)—manufacturers of his lightning rods, bifocals and stoves did not have to observe any patent rights.

Evolution of today's "Franklin" One of the first alterations to the Pennsylvanian fireplace was reduction of the size of the air-box to make more room for fuel, but this caused its passages to become clogged with dust according to one account.[3] Then the air-box was eliminated altogether, and the flue migrated from the bottom of the stove to the lower back, then to the upper back, and finally to the top of some of today's "Franklins".

The Pennsylvanian fireplace thus evolved into the familiar updraft parlor stove made in great numbers and variety in the 19th century. These stoves have been well reviewed in *Fire on the Hearth* by J. H. Peirce,[4] who has, among other things, researched old stove patents. Much effort was expended trying to improve coal and wood stoves, and many patents were granted. Indeed, most schemes for extending the usefulness of wood stoves as found today in publications like *The Mother Earth News* are revivals of ideas that occurred to our great, great grandfathers. Lying fallow in the patent office are designs for the spiral stove, the nurse stove, the egg stove, and numerous improved stoves. American ingenuity also gave birth to a patented device for "leading the flame in stoves by gauze wire" and a "reverberating plate" to improve combustion.

In 1842 Elisha Foote of Geneva, New York patented an automatic draft control based on the bimetallic strip, and ever since there has been a gradual evolution of better draft controls—the major factor in higher efficiencies of modern stoves. These will be considered after a brief, but necessary, technical interlude.

Bimetallic strip

COMBUSTION OF WOOD   About 20 per cent of the weight of air-dried wood is water. Upon heating, this absorbed water is driven off first. If the temperature rises slowly enough, the evolution of steam is completed before other changes take place. At about 300 to 400°F the wood begins

*Wood
distillation*

to break down chemically, giving rise to the volatiles composed of both common and exotic organic molecules, all of which can be burned to yield carbon dioxide, water and energy. Many of these volatiles once were commercially important products of the wood distillation industry, especially methanol (wood alcohol) and acetic acid, both of which now come from petroleum. If the temperature keeps rising, volatilization is complete at about 1000°F, leaving charcoal.

In domestic wood-burners these stages occur more or less simultaneously, although modern airtight stoves with automatic draft control can nearly duplicate industrial wood distillation if run at a slow rate. However, in home use the unburned volatiles become a nuisance and sometimes a danger. Deposition of the volatiles as creosote depends on many variables, but foremost among them are moisture content of the wood and draft. A low draft means a cool chimney, which in turn favors the condensation of steam in which some of the volatiles dissolve. In wood distillation the liquid solution formed in this way is called pyroligneous acid. It is indeed acidic and does corrode iron, even galvanized iron. On the inside of a chimney pyroligneous acid runs back toward the stove until the water is once again evaporated, leaving solid creosote behind. Even with air-dried wood there is enough residual moisture and water from the combustion reaction to form pyroligneous acid if the draft is low.

To burn the volatiles successfully requires a high temperature (over 1000°F) and oxygen, most of which is admitted

to the firebox of modern wood furnaces and boilers as sec- *Secondary*
ondary air, *i.e.* above the burning wood.[5] The rationale for *air*
this is perhaps best explained by considering what would
happen if all the air were primary, *i.e.* admitted at the base
of the fire and usually from below the grate.

In such a case most of the oxygen in the air would react
with glowing charcoal to produce carbon monoxide, carbon
dioxide and heat. The heat would stimulate production of
volatiles from the sticks above the charcoal, but they could
not burn because the atmosphere in the upper part of the
firebox would be deficient in oxygen.

That is to say: Primary draft by itself stimulates the production of volatiles, but does not provide enough oxygen for
their combustion. Secondary air inlets should be designed so
that the oxygen is well mixed with the volatiles before they
leave the firebox and are cooled. In wood-fired boilers in
electric power plants this is achieved by blowing secondary
air into the firebox through nozzles.[6]

MODERN STOVES   The most striking difference between 19th century wood stoves and current offerings is the
lack of gingerbread on most newer models, some of which
don't even look like wood stoves. Visitors need never know
that you burn wood, the fuel most likely to give you poverty
status in the eyes of the federal government.

Pictured next is an Ashley cabinet model showing the

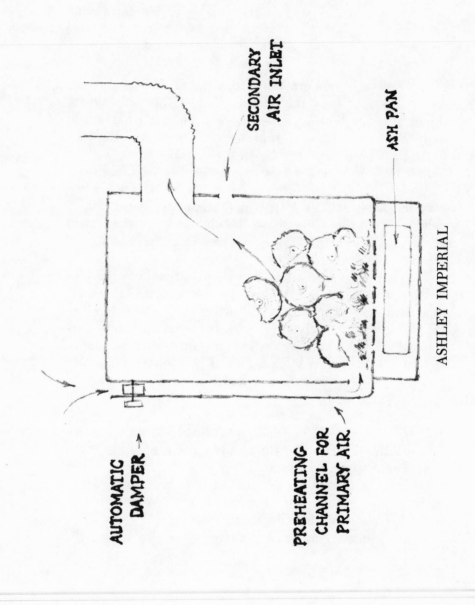

SECONDARY AIR INLET

ASH PAN

ASHLEY IMPERIAL

AUTOMATIC DAMPER →

PREHEATING CHANNEL FOR PRIMARY AIR

general flow of air through the stove. Clearly it is in the up-draft category, despite company advertisements to the contrary. Primary air flows downward in the preheating channel on the outside of the firebox, but passes across and upward through the fuel inside the firebox. This stove is a direct descendant of the airtight patented by Orr. Like Orr's stove, the body of the Ashley is of sheet metal, it is well sealed, and the primary air supply is controlled by an improved automatic damper based on a coiled bimetallic strip. Innovations are preheating of the primary draft and addition of an automatic secondary air inlet above the firebed. This is open only at lower temperatures during distillation of volatiles when secondary air is necessary. At the higher temperatures of the charcoal-burning phase the secondary air inlet closes.

Draft preheating

Preheating of the primary draft is desirable because it helps maintain a high firebox temperature, which in turn determines the extent to which the energy-liberating combustion reactions occur. Draft preheating has been incorporated into wood-fired power plants for a long time, but it is questionable how effective the Ashley preheating system actually is.

Ashleys can hold a fire for a long time and burn almost any kind of wood including white pine and aspen, and that is why their owners are so devoted and give such enthusiastic testimonials. Many Ashley owners build only one fire a year, and from then on add fuel only two or three times a day until spring.

On the other hand, Ashleys are notorious producers of creosote. At bedtime they are customarily packed full of logs and the primary draft turned down. The firebox is chilled by this big fuel load, and with only enough primary air to keep the coals glowing, the wood distillation process commences as described above, although the three phases may not be so neatly separated in time. Throughout the night, water vapor and volatiles slowly distil into a cool chimney, and pyroligneous acid is formed. Gradually this turns into solid creosote, and in the morning the householder awakens to a stove full of high quality charcoal—"the perfect fuel"—and an inflammable chimney. Turning up the primary draft then warms the house in a hurry, especially if the creosote ignites.

Creosote

To alleviate the creosote problem the Ashley Company sells its patented Downdraft Equalizer, a name not wholly appropriate, since creosote is deposited even in the absence of downdrafts. This device simply admits additional secondary air at the junction of the firebox and the flue in such a way that turbulence is promoted in the merging gas streams. Even when the flue temperature is so low that the additional air contributes nothing to combustion, it does dilute the water vapor and volatiles and thereby helps prevent the condensation of pyroligneous acid—at the expense of warm room air, however.

The ideal solution would be complete combustion of volatiles in the stove proper. One effort to achieve this elusive goal was the base-burning stove designed in 1832 by Rev.

Eliphalet Nott of Union College in Schenectady, New York.[7] Nott, like Franklin, was an avid experimenter, and his efforts led to many patents, both here and abroad. Although Dr. Nott's stoves were for coal, his base-burning magazine stove was a forerunner of the modern Riteway pictured next. The essential difference between this stove and the Ashley is the secondary chamber for combustion of volatiles communicating with the main firebox through a hole at the level of the grate. This arrangement confines the draft, and hence also the fire, to the base of the fuel charge. Thus, by virtue of the design itself, the fire cannot rise up into the whole fuel load at once. Thus there is inherent protection against uncontrolled overheating.

But the most important feature of the base-burner is the extra heating of the volatiles from passing close to the hot coals in going from the primary to the secondary combustion chamber. Being hot, the volatiles should be more completely burned in the secondary combustion chamber, and thus there should be no formation of creosote. But in practice the desired results are not achieved, for otherwise there would be no need for the "magnetic creosote inhibitor" provided with each Riteway sold.

As with almost any stove in which the draft goes in any direction other than straight up, Dr. Nott's magazine stoves smoked when opened for reloading. He therefore provided a bypass door between the top of the magazine and the exit flue. By opening this door before refueling a strong updraft was created and back-puffing avoided. Riteway stoves operate similarly.

Back-puffing of smoke is to be avoided not only because it is unpleasant to breathe, but also because it is hazardous. Since smoke consists of unburned volatiles, sudden exposure of hot smoke to atmospheric oxygen—as by opening the magazine door—may cause it to ignite and backflash, although backflashing is rare and can be avoided by refueling after the volatilization phase. But for safety, when reloading any airtight, heat the chimney first by increasing the draft for a few minutes (Franklin's trick); then close the primary draft control and open the magazine door slowly so that a good inward draft is established through it and no smoke comes out toward you.

Wood furnaces   Riteway wood furnaces are similar in design to the Riteway stove, but a blower to force the primary draft is standard equipment on the furnace. It runs only when heat is called for by a remote thermostat. A draft-inducing fan on the flue runs constantly, however. Secondary air in the furnace is preheated by passing underneath the firebox. Riteway offers wood-burning boilers too, as well as combination wood-coal-oil burners.

Another builder of wood furnaces is Perley Bell of Grafton, Vermont. Like Riteway models, his furnace is also a base-burner, but unlike the Riteway, natural draft is usually sufficient because of simpler design.

Primary air is controlled by a solenoid-operated damper that is either completely open or completely closed. When

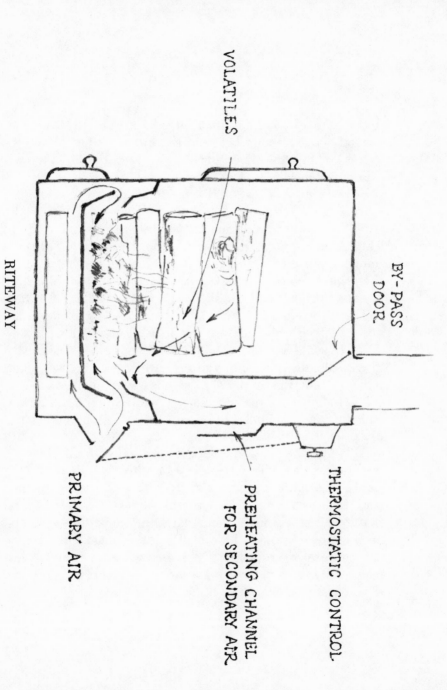

VOLATILES

BY-PASS DOOR.

RITEWAY

PRIMARY AIR

PREHEATING CHANNEL FOR SECONDARY AIR

THERMOSTATIC CONTROL

open, primary air is distributed to the fire through vents arranged symmetrically between the firebricks just above the grates. When the primary draft is shut off, the fire naturally dies down and the temperature falls. This causes the gases in the firebox to contract, and some air is drawn into the primary chamber through the secondary air port, which also supplies air to the chimney in the absence of primary draft. The incoming oxygen stimulates the fire and produces a temporary rise in temperature which causes the hot gases in the primary combustion chamber to expand into the secondary combustion chamber and block further influx of oxygen from the secondary air port. This is an excellent example of a *Negative* negative feedback system, elegant in its simplicity. The es-
feedback sence of such systems is stability and control. If the fire begins to die down, oxygen diffuses in to enliven it; if it begins to get too hot, the supply of oxygen is cut off and the fire subsides. In this way the fire is kept barely alive until heat is called for once again by the upstairs thermostat, and the primary air vent opens.

Although the magazine door is outfitted with the standard metal flap as a smoke screen, and in spite of the bypass door, smoke has ample opportunity to escape during refueling, since the furnace can hold a quarter of a cord. Bell has found that a wall of moving air eliminates the smoke problem, and he therefore installs a blower above the magazine door for use only during refueling. Both Bellway and Riteway furnaces will heat 8 or 9 room houses on two fuel loads a day in the coldest weather.

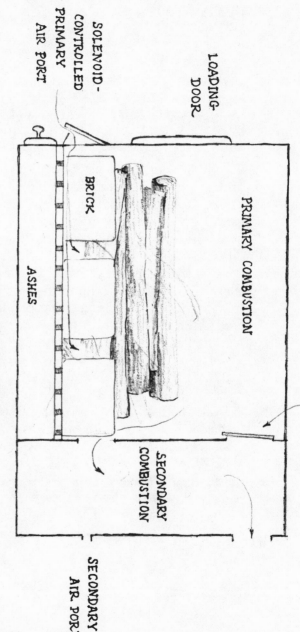

BELLWAY FURNACE

Solid and simple, this furnace relies on automatic electrical or mechanical draft control of primary air, but secondary draft control is by virtue of the design geometry itself, as in the Norwegian box stove. In warm weather the primary draft can be kept closed and the four-foot logs will burn from back to front on secondary air alone. A large automatically filling humidifier can be added and provision exists for heating household water.

SOLENOID-CONTROLLED PRIMARY AIR PORT

LOADING DOOR

BRICK

ASHES

PRIMARY COMBUSTION

BY-PASS DOOR

SECONDARY COMBUSTION

SECONDARY AIR PORT

NORWEGIAN STOVES   Ashley and Riteway stoves are sometimes said to be based on the wood distillation principle, that is, a load of fuel goes through the sequence: drying, loss of volatiles, burning of charcoal. The firebox temperature tends to rise during this sequence, and heat production is kept more or less constant by automatic reduction of the primary draft. The Jotul and Trolla stoves from Norway prove, once again, that there is more than one way to skin a cat.

Burns like a cigarette   At the end of a fuel cycle in these stoves the coals are raked toward the door to support the fresh sticks at one end. Draft is from the end rather than from below, burning the sticks evenly from one end to the other like a cigarette. This is accomplished by the addition of the baffle in the upper part of the firebox, which forces the draft into an S-shaped pattern. Because the fire is qualitatively the same throughout a fuel cycle, the heat production is even once the draft is set, and there is no need for an automatic damper.

These stoves are clearly tops in material and workmanship. They are both of heavy cast iron and sealed so well that they qualify as airtights. Both are available with or without an enamel finish—the Norwegian answer to rust.

A good "Franklin"   Jotuls are imported by Kristia Associates and Trollas by the Portland Foundry, both of Portland, Maine. These companies also offer a Norwegian version of the Franklin stove, except that the single door is tight-fitting so that the draft can be reduced to the necessary minimum for holding a fire overnight.

NORWEGIAN BOX STOVE

Here even temperature is maintained without automatic draft control by the baffle which forces the draft into an S-shaped pattern so that logs burn from one end to the other like a cigarette. Secondary air to burn the volatiles also enters through the loading door. These stoves, unsurpassed in workmanship and looks, are low enough to fit into most fireplace openings.

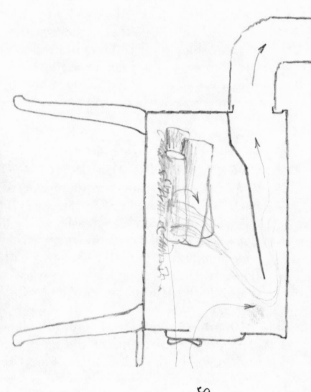

SECONDARY DRAFT

PRIMARY DRAFT

In addition the Portland Foundry imports a Trolla kitchen range for use with either coal or wood and a cast iron cousin of the Ashley with a thermostatically controlled draft. The latter stove has a cooking surface on top and a window which not only gives a fireplace effect, but also allows the operator to tell when more fuel is needed without opening the magazine door.

THE EFFICIENCY OF AIRTIGHT STOVES   The notion of efficiency is man-made and needs to be carefully defined wherever applied. In our case 100 per cent thermal efficiency corresponds to transfer of the total heat of combustion of wood to the room in which it is burned. Such a reference standard is unreal, since even with complete combustion some heat is needed to warm the chimney and create the draft. But the important thing is relative efficiencies in any case.

Unfortunately, there is very little data on wood stove efficiencies available. One of the most careful tests ever conducted was by the Northeastern Forest Experiment Station in New Haven, Connecticut in 1940 on the Char-Wood Heater, a stove designed by Professor Lauren E. Seeley of the Yale University Mechanical Engineering Department.[8] The Char-Wood was an airtight similar in design to the Riteway pictured above, except that it was of cast iron and the secondary combustion chamber was at the front of the stove instead of in back, an arrangement favoring radiation of more heat into the room and less toward the wall.

The Char-Wood registered an average efficiency of about 65 per cent, which is close to values reported for modern oil furnaces. It is doubtful, however, that commercial airtights are 65 per cent efficient under household conditions, since careful packing of the fuel magazine with small-diameter sticks is essential for efficient burning. Large voids between sticks permit air to flow in streamlines right through the firebox without coming into contact with either solid wood or volatiles. The sticks also support combustion of one another through infrared radiation, and for this reason, too, should not be very far apart.

Efficiencies* of wood-fired boilers used for generation of electricity in the Pacific Northwest have been measured at 60 per cent.[9] But that was with an engineer in constant attendance, continuous stoking of wood chips, and using preheated and forced air, both primary and secondary.

For purposes of comparison and the calculations in Chapter II we assume an efficiency of 50 per cent for modern airtights as operated in the home. Efficiency tests are laborious, but it is to be hoped that more data will become available with renewed interest in wood-burners.

50 per cent efficiency assumed

---

* *This efficiency is the fraction of the wood's fuel value actually transferred to the water in the boiler, and therefore a bit different from the efficiency as defined for a space heater.*

OTHER METAL STOVES   Aside from those already mentioned, airtight stoves with automatic draft control are also available from the King Stove Company of Sheffield, Alabama and the U. S. Stove Company of South Pittsburg, Tennessee. Both of these companies make a variety of other stoves, as does the Portland Foundry. New companies are springing up so fast that any listing of them would necessarily be incomplete.

Be cautious   Some caution is advisable when considering the products of the newer companies. Almost any iron box can hold a fire, but the secret of successful operation, aside from good fuel and a good chimney, is having control of the draft(s). Without good draft control a fire banked at bedtime may turn into a roaring blaze at 3:00 a.m. and awaken everyone in a sweat.

Among the box stoves, Franklin stoves, parlor stoves and other holdovers from the last century are many that can keep you warm and happy. They are generally cheaper than airtights and tend more toward cast iron than sheet steel. Some also have built-in humidifiers and often offer broiling and other cooking opportunities. But without exception these stoves require more attention than the airtight models discussed earlier, and for that reason are more suitable as supplementary heaters.

TILE AND SOAPSTONE STOVES   The dominant theme in American stoves has been cast iron baroque, supplanted to some extent recently by tinny modern. The constant, even warmth of the Central European tile stoves never seemed to

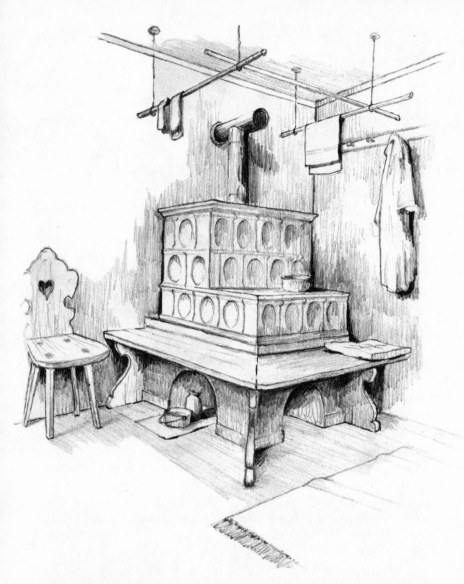

Kachelofen—building such stoves is the art of the hafner, of whom there are not many left in Europe. Bigger ones are built of bricks covered with glazed tile. The racks above are for drying clothes and the arches below can be used as brooders for chicks or for drying boots.

appeal to Americans, although they were common among some immigrant groups. Franklin speculated that the economies and comfort coming from their use would mean such an advantage to the German population in Pennsylvania that they would soon be able to buy up all the better farmland and reduce the English settlers to hired field-hands. But perhaps the Pennsylvanian fireplace prevented this and so changed the course of history.

Tile stoves were limited to small, isolated groups who managed to retain their former ways temporarily. The Moravian potters of North Carolina, for example, made tile stoves well into the 19th century, some of which had cast iron fireboxes bearing ceramic superstructures.

German stoves

The stove in the drawing is typical of those found in old German farmhouses. Note the absence of a loading door, indicating that this particular stove is fired from a hallway or adjacent room. Thus no air is drawn by the stove from the warm room itself, a fact that must indeed have meant a considerable advantage to the German settlers.

When Franklin was designing the Pennsylvanian fireplace he rejected external firing because without a constant influx of fresh air the Germans were *"obliged to breathe the same unchanged air continually, mixed with the breath and perspiration from one another's bodies, which is very disagreeable to those who have not been accustomed to it."* But Franklin objects too strongly, since ventilation could have been provided in any case, although German houses may indeed have seemed stuffy in comparison to what Franklin was used to: *"These new chimneys [referring to the new, smaller fireplaces], though they keep rooms generally free from smoke, and, the opening being contracted, will allow the door to be shut, yet, the funnel [chimney], still requiring a considerable quantity of air, it rushes in at every crevice so strongly, as to make a continual whistling or howling; and it is very uncomfortable, as well as dangerous, to sit against any such crevice. Many colds are caught from this cause only, it being safer to sit in the open street . . . Women particularly, from this cause, as they sit much in the house, get colds in the head, rheums, and defluctions, which fall into their jaws and gums, and have destroyed early many a fine set of teeth in these northern colonies."*

Note in the drawing also the wooden bench for warming aching backs and chilled spines directly. It may be correctly inferred that this stove never gets very hot. Its labyrinthian internal passageways soak up most of the fire's heat, but because of its massiveness this does not cause a great rise in temperature. Being relatively cool, the tile stove is not as good a radiator of heat as the American cast iron stove, although its greater surface area compensates somewhat. Heat is transferred to the room air slowly by direct contact, and this calls for a room free of drafts, but not so draft-free as suggested by Franklin. He must have been hypersensitive to body odors, for when consulted on how to ventilate the House of Commons, he advised that individual air outlets be installed in each M.P.'s seat so that "the personal atmospheres surrounding the members might be carried off." The English must have had plenty of soap at the time, since settlers were ferociously cutting American forests and sending potash to England.

The chief advantage of American cast iron stoves is their capacity to get hot within minutes. American houses of light wooden construction, built before the invention of plywood *Steady* and tar paper, tend to get cold at night. Under such circum- *but slow* stances a stove that on a cold morning glows dull red shortly after kindling is what's needed. On these mornings one is apt to think it a Gift of God. The forte of the tile stoves is even heat, not instant response.

American soapstone stoves, still made by the Vermont Soapstone Company of Perkinsville, are a compromise, being heavy and able to hold heat, but resembling American cast iron parlor stoves in design. Soapstone can be broken, but it will not rust, and that is why these stoves find a clientele among owners of saltwater boats. They are also quite suitable as parlor stoves. One must simply remember to start a fire in them well before the parlor is to be used.

FIREPLACES   If you have a fireplace, the best attitude *Inefficient* in the long run may be to sublimate thoughts about its ineffi- ciency and enjoy this luxury for what it does offer. Or you may try to improve its efficiency. But a fireplace is not a stove, and no matter what you do, it will never equal a good stove thermally.

In the absence of a heat-o-later, a fireplace heats the room occupants by radiation only, that is, by rays like those that bring the sun's energy to earth. Some of this radiation is absorbed by the room's walls from which heat may be transferred to room air by direct contact. But the warmth is soon lost, since the wide mouth of the fireplace allows air currents to pass into the chimney without coming close to the fire and contributing to combustion. It is easy to demonstrate the presence of these air currents by exploring the space around the fire with a smoldering stick and observing where the smoke goes.

One can reduce airflow to the chimney by use of commercially available glass screens with small draft holes at the bottom. Virtually none of the infrared radiation from the fireplace can pass through these screens, but they permit viewing the fire without serious loss of room air. They are therefore especially appropriate in rooms already heated by some other means. In any case, room heat can be significantly conserved by covering the fireplace at bedtime with a screen of metal or asbestos board. There must be a little leakage around the edges so that smoke is carried up the chimney.

Glass screens

BUYING OLD STOVES   Second-hand stoves are not as available as they once were, nor are they any longer cheap. Nevertheless, old stoves have their appeal, so here are a few pointers:

Many parlor stoves from the last century were made for coal. These were lined with firebrick because coal is a more compact fuel and often burns at a higher temperature than wood. But that in itself does not preclude the use of wood in coal stoves. Small loading doors and small fireboxes are a nuisance, however, since they mean cutting wood to very short lengths. Most wood stoves accommodate sticks at least a foot long.

The same applies to kitchen stoves. Loading doors on those intended for coal are often small, and the firebrick in the firebox takes up space that could be used for fuel. Fortunately it is fairly easy to replace bulky firebrick with smaller cast iron linings. These can be fashioned from miscellaneous pieces from the local junk yard, or, depending on make and model, be obtained commercially from companies such as the Empire Stove and Furnace Company of Albany, New York or the Atlantic Clarion Stove Company of Brewer, Maine.

Look for cracks in any second-hand stove. A crack affects not only efficiency; it can also cause smokiness and, in a kitchen range, turn baking into a very frustrating experience.

Repairing old stoves

Small cracks can be filled with furnace cement. Larger ones must be brazed (soldered at high temperature) with various copper alloys, since it is impossible to repair cast iron with ordinary welding. Brazing should not be used on any part of the firebox itself, however, because brazing alloys melt below 1600°F, and temperatures sometimes get up to 1800°F in wood-burners. Nickel welding should be used for repairs to the firebox. The result doesn't look as good as new, but the weld won't melt below 2200°F.

The Glenwood is a sturdy stove with four draft controls that will last a lifetime and then some. But wood must be cut to short lengths, and much of the heat goes to the wall behind the stove because the back gets hotter than the front.

A little rust is not an insoluble problem. Kerosene and a power drill fitted with a wire brush literally can turn a $50 stove into a $200 stove. The kerosene is used to float the rust particles so that they can be wiped away. Otherwise it is very difficult to extract them from all the nooks and crannies. Think twice before buying a stove in which internal parts are seriously rusted, especially posts, dampers, and collars in kitchen ranges.

THE CHIMNEY   Stove manufacturers provide booklets with their products giving practical information on the construction and use of chimneys. Their advice is to be heeded: don't connect more than one stove to a flue; use thimbles where stove pipe goes through a partition; don't constrict the flue anywhere along its length; and make the chimney high enough. Using nothing more than high school physics, it's easy to show that the lifting force on the hot gases in the chimney is directly proportional to the height of the chimney. The chimney is too high only when it is in danger of being toppled by high winds or when heat loss from the portion above the roof is so great that the exhaust gases are chilled at the top.

The question for most people then is whether to build a masonry chimney or buy prefabricated stainless steel sections packed with asbestos. Aside from cost (neither is cheap), the answer depends on the kind of house you have and personal preference to some extent. A massive masonry chimney in the middle of the house acts as a heat reservoir and promotes evenness of temperature. It is not coincidental that the early settlers in New England put the chimney in the middle and built the house around it. In this way they managed to recover some heat upstairs that was lost to the chimney through their outrageously inefficient fireplaces downstairs.

The advantages of the metal chimney are ease of installation and flexibility. Anyone fairly handy with tools can put one up. They are also easy to take down in case you decide that the kitchen range should go on the other side of the room after all. And if it turns out that your chimney doesn't draw well, just climb on the roof and add another section.

If the chimney must be external, Franklin pointed out it's best to put it on the south side where it is warmed by the sun and shielded from chilling north winds.

One hazard of chimneys arises from the tendency to hide them from view inside walls. A chimney exposed so that incipient failure can be detected is safer than one not easily inspected. If your chimney is an old one, and you are not sure that it is safe, inquire whether the local fire department will inspect it. If not, the standard method of checking for cracks is to build a fire, put wet newspapers over the top and then to sniff around for escaping smoke.

The best precaution against chimney fires is to burn only dry wood. But not everyone is in a position to do so, and even with dry wood, it would be foolish to gamble on never having a chimney fire. Before the development of airtight

Chimney fires

stoves a chimney fire was hard to control, and, once started, burned ferociously until all the creosote was entirely consumed. With a truly airtight system, however, the draft to the chimney is controllable, allowing one to burn the creosote out of the chimney at a moderate rate or to stop the fire altogether.

The same control can be achieved in non-airtight stoves (most kitchen ranges for example) by installing a snugly fitting damper (not the kind with holes) in the stove pipe. In an emergency this damper can cut off all air to the chimney, but not to the firebox itself—as one realizes when smoke begins to fill the house.

Chemical
sweeping
One method of preventing chimney fires is by traditional or chemical chimney sweeping. Sodium chloride is the old standby for the latter, but commercial products are calcium chloride or a mixture of sodium chloride and copper sulfate. When these salts are thrown on a hot fire fumes rise in the chimney and cause creosote to flake and fall into the fire. A spruce bough pulled through the round flue of a steel chimney will do the same thing. Heavy chains can be used on masonry chimneys.

Whatever you do with respect to fire, do it right, play it safe and sleep more peacefully. Franklin did, and then some. He inspired and helped organize the first volunteer fire company in Philadelphia, invented the lightning rod, and then, aware that others might be less cautious, had a trap door built in his roof so he could throw water on it in case his neighbor's house caught fire.

1. This and all the following quotations of Franklin are taken from *The Works of Benjamin Franklin,* Jared Sparks, ed., Townsend MacCoun, Chicago, 1882, vol. VI. The relevant essays are:

"An Account of the New-Invented Pennsylvanian Fire-Place," 1744

"On Fire," 1762

"On Ventilation—written by Mr. Small, the surgeon, but containing Dr. Franklin's Observations on the Subject"

"On the Causes and Cure of Smoky Chimneys," 1785

"Description of a new Stove for burning Pitcoal, and consuming all its Smoke," 1786

2. As late as 1860 the average American family was burning 17.5 cords annually. S. H. Schurr and B. C. Netschert, *Energy in the American Economy,* 1850-1975. Johns Hopkins Press, Baltimore, 1960, p. 49.

3. Lawrence Wright, *Home Fires Burning: The History of Domestic Heating and Cooking,* Hillary, London, 1964.

4. J. H. Peirce, *Fire on the Hearth,* Pond-Ekberg, Springfield, Massachusetts, 1951.

5. This is a development that would not have occurred to Franklin because of his incomplete, and partly erroneous, conception of fire:

"Fire penetrates bodies, and separates their parts; the air receives and carries off the parts separated, which, if not carried off, would impede the action of the fire. With the assistance therefore of a moderate current of air, the separation increases, but too violent a blast carries off the fire itself; and thus any fire may be blown out, as a candle by the breath, if the blast be proportionable."

"But, if air contributed inflammatory matter, as some have thought, then it should seem, that, the more air, the more the flame would be augmented, which beyond certain bounds does not agree with the fact."

6. Yes, wood's potential energy is still converted into electricity by the Otter Tail Power Company of Bemidji, Minnesota and the Eugene Water and Electric Board of Eugene, Oregon.

7. J. H. Peirce, loc. cit., p. 126.

8. A description of the Char-Wood Heater and preliminary test results can be found in "The Testing of Char-Wood Heaters in Connecticut," Occasional Paper no. 10, Northeastern Forest Experiment Station, A. W. Bratton, Oct. 10, 1940.

9. Otto deLorenzi, ed., *Combustion Engineering*, Combustion Engineering Company, New York, 1948, p. 12.12.

PUTTING
IT ALL
TOGETHER

IN THIS CHAPTER WE TRY TO PUT THE ELEMENTS together into a workable system. Part of our task is to rediscover many things our forefathers knew, yet we may also hope to make some improvements of our own. As inheritors of a world-view in which progress flows more or less automatically from an ever expanding and ever more wondrous technology, we must be on guard against expecting too much. Clearly the modern airtight stove, when compared to the fireplace, can be cited as one of technology's triumphs. It does not follow that giant steps of this kind are any longer possible.

The chain saw, too, makes a real difference, allowing one man to do the work of three. Thus going back to wood is not quite the same thing as going back to Ye Goode Olde Days. If the airtight stove reduces the wood needed to heat a

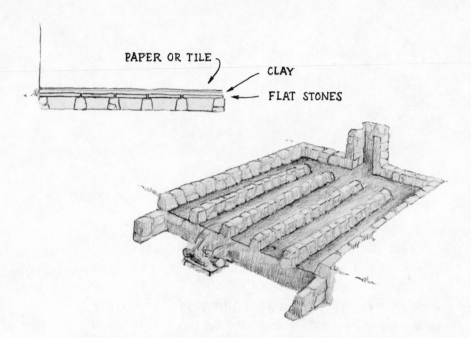

PAPER OR TILE

CLAY

FLAT STONES

With a hypocaust maximum use is made of scarce fuelwood in Korean farmhouses where the family room is warmed through the mud floor by hot gases from the kitchen fire. Four or five separate flues in the floor slope slightly upward to promote good draft and reunite in the single chimney on the opposite wall. In winter almost all activities take place in this one room. At night beds are unrolled directly on the warm floor.

Roman hypocausts were elaborately engineered, first in bath-buildings and later in houses in Germany where central heating was needed more than in sunny Italy. Hot gases issued from an adjoining furnace room into a large plenum under the baths from which they were distributed to many vertical flues in the walls to keep the frescoes dry.

house to one-quarter of that formerly required, then the combination of the chain saw and the airtight reduces the labor involved in heating with wood to about one-twelfth of what it was in the fireplace era. Modern insulation makes the ratio even more favorable. *Labor saved*

However, some of this newly gained advantage has been undermined by an abundance of cheap energy, which has helped us forget the basics. Thus we find Texas ranch houses in Minnesota and air conditioning in Vermont where shade trees are removed by builders for their own convenience. We start, therefore, with the fundamentals.

WHERE TO PUT WOOD-BURNERS   Hot air rises. Hence wood-burners should go toward the bottom of a house. The lower the wood-burner and the higher the chimney, the better the draft and the more useful the heat in general. Two-story houses favor better use of the heat energy liberated in stoves and furnaces, and that is no doubt why they are common in cold climates. The ranch house makes sense in Texas, not Minnesota.

For conservation of heat the surface area of the house should be minimal relative to the volume. Geometrically this suggests a spherical house, but a cube, the next best form, is easier to build and live in.

A stove on the first level warms the floor above and takes the chill off the upstairs rooms. In Roman and Korean hypocausts ("to burn below") this principle is carried to an extreme in that the lower space is reduced to a horizontal or slightly sloping chimney and the room above is kept warm through the floor.

If you want more heat in an upstairs bedroom than comes through the floor by conduction, a hole in the floor to allow an upward current of warm air may be preferable to a stove in the bedroom itself, since upstairs stoves are apt to be smoky because of short flue length.

Put stove in middle

Besides being downstairs, stoves should be toward the middle of the house and away from outside walls. This is where they are put anyway, if the chimney is in the middle where it belongs. With the stove in the middle, circulation of air in the room is as shown. Air warmed by the stove goes up along the inside wall and falls along the chilly outside wall. But before getting to the outside wall the air gives up part of its heat to the floor above for second-hand use.

VENTILATION AND HUMIDITY   How much ventilation is desirable is a matter of personal taste, depending to some extent on how often your family and friends bathe. Taking combustion air from the heated room itself draws in an equivalent amount of cold air from outside, usually through cracks around windows and doors. With an efficient airtight stove this air needed to feed the fire is less than that recommended for health and comfort, according to people who study such things.

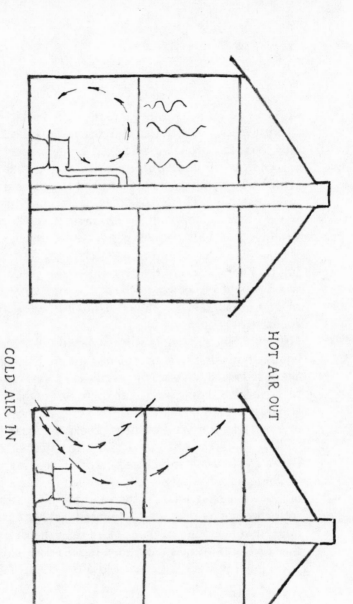

AIR CIRCULATION IN A WELL-
BUILT HOUSE HELPS TO HEAT
THE UPSTAIRS

COLD AIR IN   UNWANTED DRAFTS CARRY
              HEAT AWAY

HOT AIR OUT

As an example, consider a room with a relatively large rate of heat loss—an uninsulated living room 13 x 22 x 8½ feet. If this room has brick walls backed by tar paper, wood sheathing and plaster, a weather-stripped door and storm windows, it will take about 16,000 BTU per hour to heat it in zero-degree weather.[1] These 16,000 BTU (from 5 to 7 pounds of wood) can be supplied by an airtight stove with ease. Assuming that half the oxygen taken into the stove passes through the firebox and into the chimney without ever entering into combustion,[2] the amount of air needed to burn this wood would be less than the recommended ventilation rate of 750 cubic feet per hour, assuming three people in the room.[3]

If this were the whole story, we could conclude that taking combustion air from the heated room itself represents no thermal loss, since normal ventilation represents a bigger air turnover rate anyway. But if there are cracks to supply the stove with its 300 cubic feet per hour, chances are there are other cracks too. And if these cracks are near the ceiling as well as the floor, unwanted and often unsuspected influx of cold air will occur as pictured on the preceding page.

Heat-robbing drafts

These heat-robbing drafts can account for a large fraction of the total heat loss. In the example above the ventilation rate through cracks was estimated at 3745 cubic feet per hour, that is, about 12 times more than the draft required by the stove and 5 times more than required for comfort.

In general it is easier to build a tight house and then provide for the necessary ventilation intentionally than it is to reduce unwanted ventilation in a drafty house. But, unfortunately, many people are already in the second situation and face the task of plugging leaks until the right ventilation rate has been reached. When the room air begins to get stuffy you know your efforts in this direction have been successful.

It should be mentioned, too, that unwanted ventilation is *Low* even more undesirable than has so far been suggested, since *humidity* incoming air, being relatively cold, contains little water vapor. (At 70°F, for example, air can hold eight times more moisture than at 12°F.) This accounts for dryness of houses in winter, which is objectionable because it promotes loss of body heat through evaporation from the skin and respiratory tract. At 70°F and a relative humidity of 45 per cent as much as one-quarter of the body's heat loss is by evaporation, assuming normal clothing and normal activity.[4] Evaporative heat loss can be reduced to almost nothing by raising the humidity of the air, but at considerable cost in energy if done by tea kettle or humidifier. The better way is to put a stop to excessive draftiness.

In the development of stoves it was gradually realized that the key to greater thermal efficiency was reducing the draft to the minimum amount consistent with effective combustion. Today household thermal efficiency can often be significantly enhanced by reducing ventilation to the minimum amount consistent with comfort. If your throat feels parched in the winter, your house is too drafty.

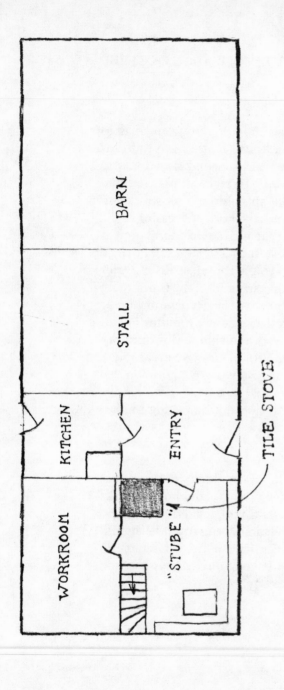

BAVARIAN FARMHOUSE

The hallway is big enough for a stack of wood, and the tile stove in the heated room (Stube, whence the English words stove and stew) is fired from the hallway and not the room itself, leaving dirt and bark outside the living area. By exposing one face of the stove in the neighboring workroom, it too is kept warm. The kitchen is heated only by the cookstove and only when in use. Note that the chimney and both stoves are in the middle of the house where they should be. Warm cows in the attached barn help to retard heat loss from the house.

The ventilation rate required to support combustion in a good stove is so low that external firing provides no advantage, at least on this score. But on grounds of cleanliness it can be recommended. Wood is a dirty fuel in one sense; ashes make dust, and dirt is inevitably brought into the house with logs and sticks. If your stove back-puffs (heaven forbid—you've done something wrong!) the dirt problem can be serious, both in the house and in your lungs. External firing goes a long way toward relieving this nuisance, except in the hallway from which the stoves are fired. But in old German farmhouses that was dirty anyway, because it served as the mudroom too. (Incidentally, if you decide to adopt the German method, be sure to make the hallway door big enough so that a cart or wheelbarrow loaded with wood can be brought right into the hall.)

WASTED ENERGY   About half of the potentially useful energy of wood goes up the chimney. In a house burning 8 cords per winter, this amounts to a waste of 100,000,000 BTUs annually—enough for the rest of your household energy requirement, including your compact car, for a full year.

It is doubtful that the basic efficiency of home wood-burners can be improved much more, since there are limitations inherent in the irregular shape and size of wood fuel. Blowing very fine sawdust into the combustion chamber in an intimate mixture with air might improve furnace efficiencies, but clearly this is feasible only on a large scale, in power plants for example.

When stoves are run at a low rate, combustion is incomplete, as indicated by the formation of creosote. At a high rate exhaust gases carry away too much heat, as is obvious from the wavy appearance of the air above chimneys. From the point of view of efficiency, the answer to the first loss is to burn the creosote in the chimney; but this represents very little thermal gain unless there is a way of getting heat out of the stack and back into the house. We concentrate, therefore, on how to do just this.

THE EXTENDED STOVEPIPE   When churches were heated with wood, the stove was usually right in the middle and the stovepipe was suspended for a distance of 20 feet or so above the heads of the congregation before reaching the chimney. In a lofty room that was heated only one morning out of seven, this extra length of pipe must have contributed significantly to the comfort of the faithful, for when connected to a very hot stove it was no doubt an excellent heat radiator. The Shakers, who emphasized utility in all their implements, added *bona fide* heat exchangers to their stoves and then doubled the stovepipe too.

But long stovepipes are not without problems. If the crimped ends of individual sections point toward the chimney, any pyroligneous acid that forms can run back down and out through the joints. In the worst case this will dry into creosote on the outside of the pipe, catch fire, fall to the floor and burn the house down. In the best case it will impart a pungent odor to the air and mess up the floor a bit.

To avoid this problem the formation of pyroligneous acid usually can be prevented by burning only dry wood and, to be absolutely certain, by installing the stovepipe with the crimped ends toward the stove so that no liquid can run out. *Crimped ends toward stove* This latter is contrary to the usual advice which alleges that our method lets smoke out into the room. Nonsense: as long as the chimney is drawing, air flows inward through any cracks in the stovepipe, a fact put to use in the Ashley Downdraft Equalizer.

In modern houses stoves will in most cases be entirely adequate without extending the stovepipe. If the stove must be far from the chimney and a long stovepipe is unavoidable, it should be strapped securely in place, since it is apt to oscillate wildly if it is loose and catches fire. This could cause a joint to come apart. We leave the reader to contemplate the consequences and move on.

HEAT EXCHANGERS A heat exchanger is a device especially designed to transfer heat from one fluid to another. In our case we wish to transfer heat from hot flue gases to some useful enterprise in the house, either space or water

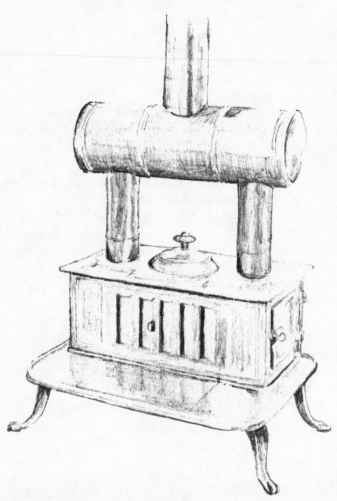

This stove with heat exchanger has two flues and a horizontal cylinder above the stove provide extra surface area for radiating more heat into the room. This stove is a fancy model no longer made, but the same improvement can be added to almost any stove by putting a steel drum between two sections of stovepipe. The drum becomes an oven by welding a metal box into it and adding a door.

heating. Significant dollar savings can be realized either way, but transferring heat to water is easier. Thus car engines are more often cooled by water than air. When air is used as a coolant, its inferior thermal properties (low thermal conductivity and low specific heat) must be compensated for by increasing the surface area where the heat exchange occurs. In a chain saw or Volkswagen engine this is done with fins.

When heating room air with hot flue gases the necessary surface area can be provided by breaking the flue up into many tubes. In one such heat exchanger designed especially for wood stoves the tubes are 7/8-inch in diameter, and the room air to be heated is blown by a small fan across the array of tubes set in the stovepipe. To get the best efficiency, the tubes should have a small cross-section, but the smaller they are, the oftener the whole assembly must be dismantled and cleaned. According to the inventor this device increases the efficiency of a Franklin stove from 15 to 60 per cent.[5]

Otherwise wasted energy

HOT WATER   In homes where a wood fire is kept going all winter, heat that escapes up the chimney can be used to preheat water before it goes into a conventional heater. This will reduce the bills for household energy significantly.

The water coming into our house is at about 40°F. It goes first to a 52-gallon tank where it is heated to 80°-100°F in the chimney before going to a small electric heater where the temperature is raised to 120°F. Thus the chimney preheater does at least half the job and reduces the electric bill correspondingly (by about \$10/month).

Water from the bigger tank is heated in a one-inch straight copper pipe about six feet long installed inside the 7 x 7-inch tile-lined flue of a masonry chimney. Iron pipe would not be suitable, because any pyroligneous acid deposited will corrode iron. An iron water loop in the firebox is safe because no acid solution is formed there. At our house soot does build up on the copper pipe in the chimney but not to the extent of preventing a reasonable rate of heat transfer—although this would not hold true where creosote production is excessive.

Soldered joints in the copper should be avoided. We used threaded brass fittings to make right angles at top and bottom. In case of a chimney fire, steam could cause the pressure to get dangerously high, so a relief valve should be installed to discharge safely if the emergency arose.

We tried bendable copper tubing in the chimney at first, but it did not permit sufficiently sharp bends and it bulged out into the center of the flue, so that flue cleaning was difficult.

None of the system outlined above reflects detailed scientific reasoning. The tanks used were what we happened to have on hand. But the system does work, and it required no unusual materials or skills to install.

We have reservations about home-made water heating loops built right in the firebox, because of the banging they

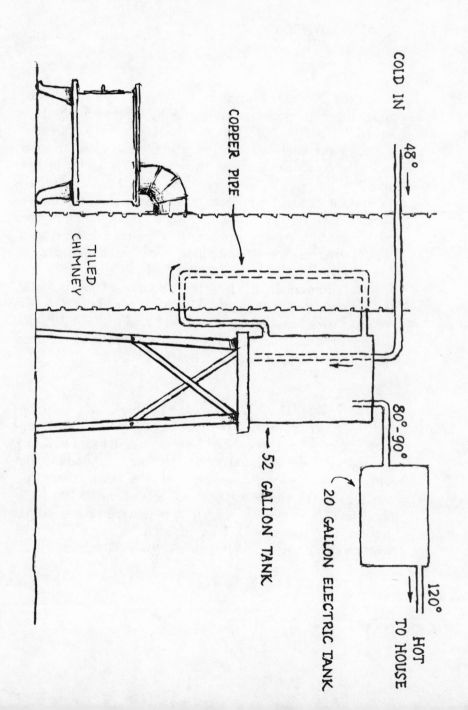

would get from throwing wood in. The old cast iron "coils", apparently no longer manufactured, were virtually indestructible and fitted snugly out of the way.

Kitchen stove

The wood kitchen range with built-in hot water reservoir is a great convenience, though it takes hours to heat up. But the range does more than heat water. In the old days it brought people together and was the basic element in a whole way of life, performing functions since then taken over by separate appliances: coffee percolator, toaster, clothes drier, iron, electric broiler, oven, humidifier, dustbin and electric blanket (by heating bedwarmers). In subtle ways it encouraged more healthful and more enjoyable food. If the stove was hot anyway, why not put bread dough in the warming oven or on the hearth to rise? And why not do more baking? It also demanded certain daily chores and enforced its own discipline, since missed by some.

A FINAL WORD   Good luck! This book ends here, but the uses of wood do not. Your car, for example, could be converted to wood fuel for about $300 and some inconvenience. The latter is determining when gasoline is abundant, but when it is scarce, wood-powered vehicles become more attractive. By the end of 1942 90 per cent of the 75,000 registered motor vehicles in Sweden were powered by wood-gas

Gasogen

generators ("gasogens"). The gasogen is basically a tank where sawdust, wood chips, or charcoal is burned with a

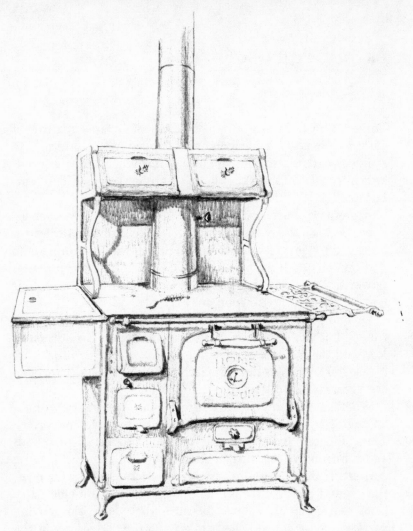

The Home Comfort (or any good kitchen stove) is a fundamental element in a way of life with a name well-chosen. Above are warming ovens, or warming closets, for raising dough and warming plates. The water reservoir can be right or left, but the firebox is always on the left. Lacking automatic control, evenness of temperature in the oven depends on the massiveness of the stove, the cook's skill, and the dedication of the wood cutter. A slab of soapstone in the bottom of the oven helps keep the temperature steady. On top the temperature varies from place to place, so it's usually possible to find just the right spot whatever the dish.

limited supply of oxygen to yield an 80-octane mixture of carbon monoxide, hydrogen and nitrogen. After filtering, to remove particulates, this mixture is introduced into a standard internal combustion engine through a modified carburetor.[6]

A gasogen, once installed, allows considerable independence, because it can also be put to use charging batteries for household electricity—easily enough for water pump, radio and one or two light bulbs. On a tractor a gasogen provides power for anything that can be connected to the drive shaft —a saw for cutting firewood, for example.

Of course a wood-fired steam engine can also do these things, but the efficiency of the steam engine is notoriously low, and the internal combustion engine is so ubiquitous that a gasogen seems preferable. Carbon monoxide and hydrogen are hazardous, but then so is gasoline.

Direct energy conversion   Wood's heat can be turned directly into electricity without an engine by use of thermoelectric or thermionic converters. These devices are based on electronic properties of metals and semiconductors. Just heating them produces an electric current. If these were less sensitive to temperature changes, they would be ideal for production of home-made electricity from waste chimney heat, because they have no moving parts. They have been used already with wood stoves in the Soviet Union to power radios in remote areas.[7] In the United States they are being developed in connection with military and space programs. In one application a thermoelectric converter is heated by a rocket's exhaust gases to generate electric power for the guidance system. (In a military rocket a long lifetime presumably is not of primary concern.)

Wood can also be made into fodder for cattle and even food for man. It can be converted into alcohol and is drunk by the Swedes and Germans in Aquavit. Organic chemists have not yet really begun to apply their art to wood, but there is no doubt that wood can, in principle, furnish all the organic chemicals that now come from petroleum. *Wood potentials*

For most of us, however, wood will remain a structural material, a source of paper and a fuel for the fireplace, stove and furnace, at least for a while. We must, in the next few decades, learn more precisely the limits to our exploitation of the forest. We must learn to make more complete use of the wood we do harvest. We should do even better. We should restore to productivity the millions of acres of former forestland that we, the human species, have turned into wasteland already.

It seems easier to destroy in greed or to adopt the hands-off attitude of the sentimentalist than to establish a harmonious relationship with the forest. That is our task. The forest is, after all, the Earth's major contact with "the Great Giver of warmth to our system."

1. *Guide and Data Book, 1963,* American Society of Heating, Refrigerating and Air-Conditioning Engineers, p. 456.

2. In the Char-Wood tests mentioned previously one-third of the oxygen taken in did not support combustion, presumably because of channeling, i.e., it passed through the firebox in streamlines without coming in contact with solid wood or volatiles.

3. This is based on the ASHRAE guideline of 240 cubic feet per person. *Guide and Data Book, 1962,* p. 799.

4. Ref. 1, p. 108.

5. *Alternative Sources of Energy,* Feb. 1974, p. 24.

6. The gasogen and many other applications of wood are discussed in an unusually intelligent way by Egon Glesinger, in *The Coming Age of Wood,* Simon and Schuster, N. Y., 1949. The U. S. Forest Service was called upon during World War II to study gasogens in connection with the China campaign and issued a report, N. R1463, giving details of construction. This report is now hard to get, but information is available. See, for example, *Alternative Sources of Energy,* July 1973, p. 23.

7. A. F. Joffe, *Scientific American,* Nov. 1958, p. 31.

Readers of this book may wish to read three other Garden Way books on closely related subjects: *New Low-Cost Sources of Energy for the Home,* by Peter Clegg; *Your Energy-Efficient House,* by Anthony Adams, and *Methanol and Other Ways Around the Gas Pump,* by John Ware Lincoln.

INDEX